Comparing Crime Data in Europe
Official Crime Statistics and Survey Based Data

Philippe Robert (ed.)

Comparing Crime Data in Europe
Official Crime Statistics and Survey Based Data

Contributions from Marcelo F. Aebi,
Bruno Aubusson de Cavarlay,
Sandrine Haymoz,
Mike Hough,
Martin Killias,
Philippe Lamon,
Paul Norris,
Joachim Obergfell-Fuchs,
Philippe Robert,
Giovanni Sacchini,
Jan Van Dijk,
Karin Wittebrood,
Renée Zauberman

This edited book is the outcome of a seminar held within a Coordination Action *Assessing Deviance, Crime and Prevention in Europe (CRIMPREV, www.crimprev.eu)* funded by the European Commission (contract 028300 under FP6) and coordinated by the Groupe européen de recherches sur les normativités (GERN, Centre national de la recherche scientifique, CNRS).

CRIMPREV

VUBPRESS

Criminological Studies

In this series studies are published which contribute significantly to the development of the criminological sciences, through either theoretical elaborations, empirical research or criminal policy discussions.
Studies originating from other scientific disciplines can also be considered if they are relevant to the criminological domain.
The editorial board consists of academics from the criminological research institutes of the Vrije Universiteit Brussel (VUB) and the Universiteit Gent (UG).
All manuscripts are reviewed by at least two referees.

Cover design: Koloriet, Leefdaal
Book design: Style, Hulshout
Print: Flin Graphic Group, Oostkamp

VUBPRESS is an imprint of ASP nv
(Academic and Scientific Publishers nv)
Ravensteingalerij 28
B-1000 Brussels
Tel. ++ 32 2 289 26 50
Fax ++ 32 2 289 26 59
E-mail info@vubpress.be
www.vubpress.be

ISBN 978 90 5487 589 5
NUR 824
Legal Deposit D/2009/11.161/048

Contents

Introduction

Philippe Robert, Renée Zauberman

The second half of the 20th century has witnessed a watershed in the systematic study of crime. Until then, crime estimates were locked up in an administrative monopoly: the only available figures resulted from counting the activities of various criminal justice agencies. By contrast, from then on, alternative measurement methods were developed based on general population surveys, which severed the crime estimates' dependency on the operation of the police or the courts.

The most important of them bear upon victimisation and sense of insecurity and have become the standard procedure for studying crime in those countries who can afford them. Secondly, self-reported crime and deviance surveys, which actually appeared as an earlier innovative development in the study of crime, are nowadays blooming as well for gaining knowledge in the field of juvenile delinquency and above all of substance use and school violence.

To be comprehensive, mention should also be made of the use as alternative measurement tools of a variety of public statistics, whose primary aim is not the estimation of crime and which do not depend on the operation of the criminal justice system: statistics on causes of death, hospital admissions, or various 'cost of crime' estimates...

However, widening the range of the measurement tools used will only be fruitful if their consideration proceeds beyond mere juxtaposition, towards genuine comparison.

Not that this is an easy task. The naïve idea has to be abandoned that all this estimates are of the same nature and as such directly comparable, as if different accountants could separately perform the same calculation.

Actually, every measurement is partial and each operates within a distinct perspective. Each one is the result of a labelling process by a distinct actor: in the self-reported delinquency survey, the perpetrator recognises a criminal nature in some of his/her behaviour; in the victim survey, the victim labels some of the misadventures suffered as offences; in crime records, the police officer suspects that some of the incidents detected or brought to his/her attention might constitute offences and should therefore be referred to the judge. Only the latter is invested with the constitutional power to decide – in accordance with particular procedural forms – whether an actual situation corresponds with the abstract provisions of the criminal law, but conversely all those social actors – professionals or laymen – who play a part in submitting cases to him have made provisional judgements like 'it seems to me that there is an offence here...' Administrative statistics and surveys are the bottom line expression of these labelling processes, of which each one is partial: there is not such thing as a view from the outer space allowing the observer to be content with a single source[1]. Whence the necessity of comparison.

Besides, each type of data has its own limitations. As they measure crime control activities, public criminal statistics are not necessarily the right yardstick to measure criminality. Fairly adequate with respect to juvenile delinquency or cannabis use, a self-reported crime survey is barely serviceable when it comes to economic/financial or organised crime. As to victimisation surveys, they are of no use for victimless crime, nor for crimes entailing participation or complicity of the victim nor for offences whose definition is too complex to be explored in a general population survey. By contrast, such surveys are well suited for various types of non-lethal assaults, for thefts, burglaries, vandalism against private property. A consensus gradually emerged that the best stance for measuring crime lay in confronting the largest possible range of data, so as to perform a kind of triangulation[2]. Without a term of comparison, an isolated data means nothing or worse, can be made to mean anything.

Obviously, as none of the data bases is exhaustive, the comparison can each time only bear upon those portions of the data that overlap. Moreover this approach entails fine-tuned adjustments of the data so as to make them comparable with each other.

Still, the game is worth the candle. The comparison allows a sort of mutual criticism between the different sources of data, which helps determining both the scope and the limitations of each. Beyond mere counting, the comparison also sheds light on the strategies and behaviours of the various actors involved, be it victims and their decision to report or not what happened to them to public institutions like the police, or professionals like the police officers and their way of handling the information brought to their attention.

Comparison between official crime statistics and survey based data has been addressed in a Coordination Action called *Assessing Deviance, Crime and Prevention in Europe* (CRIMPREV) and funded by the European Commission, within FP6.

1. Robert, 2005, 94.
2. Robert, 2005, 94.

More specifically, this topic is one of those that have been addressed by a workpackage of this Coordination Action devoted to *Methodology and Good Practices*.

I. The methodology and good practices workpackage

The aim of this Workpackage was to deliver a synthetic review of the most significant knowledge tools in the field of crime and of their use
This entailed:
- the mapping of the European situation,
- the recognition of good as well as bad practices,
- opening the way to European comparisons.

During the last half-century, new and powerful tools emerged for the knowledge of crime. They have in common to free themselves from the institutional data in which the study of crime had traditionally closeted itself. Not only have these instruments renewed, even if only partially, the academic knowledge of crime, but they have a high potential as decision-making aids.

Yet, they have been initiated under varying circumstances across Europe and their mastering is unequally distributed, the number of confirmed specialists being quite small. Consequently, their use is not always appropriate and users outside the academic sphere have often only limited knowledge of their potential.

This makes room within CRIMPREV for a Workpackage devoted to a review of the most significant operations of these instruments in the main European countries, in the hope of establishing and circulating both a state of knowledge and a catalogue of good practices in the field.

The workpackage is under the joint responsibility of an academic centre, the French *Centre de recherches sociologiques sur le droit et les institutions pénales (CESDIP)*, a professor at the *Universidad central de Barcelona*, a European network of local communities sharing urban safety concern and programmes: the European Forum for urban safety (EFUS) and an Italian regional organisation coordinating local safety programmes (*Città Sicure*). This makes this workpackage an interface between the academic and public policies spheres.

Four methods have been selected:
- general population surveys on victimisation and insecurity,
- general population surveys on self-reported crime and deviance,
- comparisons between survey-based data and others based on institutional sources, like police statistics,
- evaluative research on crime prevention and safety policies.

For each of these methods, we have proceeded according to a six-phase protocol:

- phase 1: elaboration of a report grid; selection of a general rapporteur in charge of synthesising the information collected; and of rapporteurs – a half-dozen per topic – in charge of drawing up the state of knowledge and usage in different countries where the method is sufficiently developed. Of course, given problems of availability of the approached experts, we could not cover them all. We were not aiming at exhaustiveness but rather at presenting a reasonably representative selection of what is being done in the European zone, especially in the principal countries;
- phase 2: drafting by each rapporteur of a review pertaining to the country or zone of which she/he is in charge and circulation of these drafts among all rapporteurs;
- phase 3: meeting of all rapporteurs, national and general, with the promoters of the workshop in a seminar where the reports are presented and discussed;
- phase 4: drafting by the general rapporteur of a synthesis of the reports and discussions;
- phase 5: validation of this document by the workpackage promoters and dissemination in the form of a 50-page booklet in English and French, published by the FESU;
- phase 6: publication of all the contribution in two volumes, one in English, the second in French, both edited by a member of the steering group of the workpackage.

Three first volumes have already been published in this series in 2008 and 2009, based on the first workshops of the workpackage: Zauberman R., (Ed.), *Victimisation and Insecurity in Europe ; a review of Surveys and their use;* Zauberman R., (Ed.), *Self-Reported Crime and Deviance Studies in Europe; Current State of Knowledge and Review of Use;* Robert Ph., (Ed.), *Evaluating Safety and Crime Prevention Policies in Europe.*

II. The workshop on the comparison between Official Crime Statistics and Survey Based Data

The team formed for this workshop comprised:

- Sandrine Haymoz (*Universität Zurich*), Marcelo Aebi (*Université de Lausanne*), Martin Killias (*Universität Zurich*), Philippe Lamon (*Université de Lausanne*), for Switzerland,

- Bruno Aubusson de Cavarlay (*Centre de recherches sociologiques sur le droit et les institutions pénales* – CESDIP – CNRS, U. Versailles Saint Quentin and Department of Justice), for France,
- Mike Hough (King's College) and Paul Norris (Scottish Centre for Crime and Justice Research), for the United Kingdom,
- Joachim Obergfell-Fuchs (*Kriminologischer Dienst Baden-Württemberg*), for Germany,
- Giovanni Sacchini (*Città sicure, Regione Emilia-Romagna*), for Italy,
- Karin Wittebrood (*Sociaal en Cultureel Planbureau*, SCP) for the Netherlands,
- For the general report, Jan Van Dijk (*Universiteit Tilburg),*
- Philippe Robert, Renée Zauberman (*Centre de recherches sociologiques sur le droit et les institutions pénales* – CESDIP), Amadeu Recasens i Brunet (*Universitat central de Barcelona*), Anabel Rodriguez Basanta (*Generalitat de Catalunya*), Michel Marcus (European Forum for Urban Safety – EFUS) formed the core group.

In January 2008, the national rapporteurs received a letter commissioning the work from the steering committee of the workpackage and submitted their report in July 2008. After this a seminar, chaired by Philippe Robert, was held in Barcelona and was attended by the core group, the general rapporteur and the national rapporteurs during a three-day session in September 2008, in order to present and discuss the reports, and draw cross-national lessons.

This constituted the basis for the final report, which was first published as a separate English-French booklet (Van Dijk, 2009).

The present publication comprises it together with the national reports. Beside this English publication, this book in will also be published in French (Robert, 2009) in the subseries *Déviance et Société* at L'Harmattan (Paris). Both publications have been edited by Philippe Robert ; Renée Zauberman has revised the translations.

References

ROBERT PH., 2005, *Sociologie du crime,* Paris, La Découverte.

ROBERT PH., (Dir.), 2009, *Mesurer la délinquance en Europe : comparer statistiques officielles et enquêtes*, Paris, L'Harmattan.

VAN DIJK J., 2009, *Approximating the Truth about Crime; Comparing crime data based on general population surveys with police figures of recorded crimes/Approcher la vérité sur la délinquance: comparer les données d'enquêtes aux statistiques policières*, Paris, Forum européen pour la sécurité urbaine.

Approximating the truth about crime

Comparing crime data based on general population surveys with police figures of recorded crimes

Jan Van Dijk

Both men had spent their professional lives working for the police and thus had long ago learned the sovereign truth of crime statistics: to the degree that the process of reporting a crime is made difficult and time-consuming, the numbers of reported crimes will diminish

Donna Leon, *The Girl of his Dreams*, London, William Heinemann, 2008

I. Subject matter

Since their first publication, police figures of recorded crimes are known to suffer from several inbuilt limitations. First, they reflect only crimes known to police forces, missing the so called 'dark numbers of crime', the crimes that are never reported to or detected by the police. Police figures are said to reflect just the tip of the iceberg of true crime. Second, police figures are strongly affected by the scale and effectiveness of policing activities. Trend data may therefore not necessarily reflect trends in actual crime but trends in policing efforts or priorities instead. In addition, official police figures are strongly affected by recording policies and practices of the police. They are therefore susceptible to possible manipulation and misrepresentation for political purposes. Finally, police figures in most countries are still mostly based on aggregate statistics and therefore cannot provide information on the characteristics of the incidents including of the victims involved.

Crime victimisation surveys are interview-based surveys among samples of the general public about personal experiences with crime, regardless of whether they have been reported to the police or not. The surveys were introduced as a means to produce estimates of the numbers of crimes that are produced independently from administrative data of the police. They were supposed to produce statistics of crime that include the 'dark numbers' and are not distorted by investigative efforts of the police or variable practices of police recording.

Victimisation surveys have undoubtedly improved statistical information on crime and they are generally recognised as a cornerstone of empirical criminology. Victimisation surveys, however, also suffer from several inherent limitations, as will be discussed in more detail below. Survey-based estimates of crime cannot be taken at face value either. From the outset we want to emphasise that searching for a measure of the true measure of crime is like searching for the Holy Grail. All sources of statistical information about crime reflect social constructions of the phenomenon under study. In the case of police statistics the figures reflect the crime problem as construed by law enforcement agencies and politicians, prosecutors or judges supervising their work. Police figures give us the official or statist view of the problem of crime. Crime victimisation surveys reflect crime problems as perceived and memorised by samples of ordinary citizens. These perceptions might be erroneous from a legal perspective. Both social constructions are liable to be biased in their own special ways.

Comparisons between the results of victimisation surveys with statistics of police recorded crime have initially been conducted in the hope to determine the dark number of crime and to arrive at the 'true numbers of crime'. This analytical approach has been especially prominent in the USA where the national victimisation survey was specifically launched with the view of monitoring and, where necessary correcting, the national police figures (Lynch, Addington, 2007). The National Crime (Victims) Survey (NCVS) was set up as a parallel system of the Uniform Crime Reporting System. For this reason the selection of types of crime covered and the operational concepts used in the questionnaires of the NCVS conform as closely as possible to those in the Uniform Crime Reporting System of the country. Typically, the key results of the NCVS have always been published in the form of estimated absolute numbers of crimes committed. These estimated absolute numbers could be superficially compared by any reader with the annual police figures published by the Federal Police. In line with the key objective of the surveys to monitor police figures, the questionnaire includes no questions on attitudes of the public concerning crime as is common in European surveys. Another characteristic of the NCVS is its exclusive focus on national crime trends, ignoring local variation or cross-national comparisons.

Over the years numerous in depth studies on concurrence between the two series have been conducted in the USA (for overviews see Bidermann, Lynch, 1991; Lynch, Addington, 2007). The main conclusion of these studies is that such comparisons are fraught with so many methodological problems that especially comparisons between the two alternative measures of the level of crime are hardly feasible. The original objective of determining the true level of crime seems to have been abandoned. Also, analyses of concurrence nowadays tend to focus on *change estimates* rather than on *level estimates*. Studies on convergence or divergence of the two sources are now generally seen as an analytical tool to better understand the factors determining how the two systems produce crime statistics. In a review of the issues, Lynch and Addington (2007) argues that police figures of recorded crime and survey results should be seen as complementary to each other. Both offer valuable and unique information about crime problems. In their view concurrence analysis can help to identify the relative strengths and weaknesses of both statistical series as indicators of different aspects of the crime problem.

In Europe, the first crime victim surveys were developed not by statisticians but by criminologists working for either government-funded research institutes as in The Netherlands, United Kingdom, Poland or France, or by universities (*e.g.* in Germany and Switzerland[1]) (Zauberman, 2008a & b). The criminological outlook of the first European surveys is reflected in their methodologies. The first European studies typically focused on measuring volume crime as perceived by the public using definitions and concepts taken from colloquial language rather than from national legislation (*e.g.* the offences of car vandalism, pickpocketing or consumer fraud). European surveys typically also included extended sets of questions on fear of crime and opinions about police performance or sentencing. Unlike the NCVS in the USA, most reports on European surveys refrain from presenting estimated absolute numbers of crime. European reports typically present prevalence and incidence rates of victimisation per 100,000 as their key findings.

In order to make tentative comparisons with the statistics of crimes recorded by the police, results of European surveys must be adjusted *post hoc* to better approach the legal definitions used in police administrations (the identifications of comparable subsets in both series). Subsequently, incidence rates per 100,000 persons or households must be 'grossed up' to arrive at estimates of the absolute numbers of crimes experienced by the population (Van Dijk, Steinmetz, 1980; Wittebrood, Junger, 2002; Lagrange *et al.*, 2004; Allan, Ruparel, 2006). The comparisons in Europe are further complicated by the fact that national figures of police-recorded crimes are often less rigorously standardised than in the USA. In England

1. In Germany the first surveys were conducted by academic scholars such as Stephan, Schwind, Kury and Pfeiffer (Stephan, 1976; Schwind *et al.*, 1975; Schwind *et al.*, 1978; Schwind *et al.*, 1889; Kury, 1991; Wetzels, Pfeiffer, 1996). All Swiss National Crime Victim Surveys were conducted by the School of Criminal Sciences of the University of Lausanne and directed by Martin Killias.

and Wales, a system of Uniform Crime Reporting has only recently been introduced. In other countries uniform crime statistics are still hardly available at the federal level at all (*e.g.* in Belgium and Switzerland). If American researchers have found such comparisons to be a daunting challenge, in the European context the exercise can be characterised as a 'mission impossible'. After initial attempts to calculate dark numbers in Germany (Stephan, 1976; Schwind *et al.*, 1978) and The Netherlands (Buikhuisen, 1974; Fiselier, 1978; Van Dijk, Steinmetz, 1980), interest waned. For this reason the European literature on the issues of convergence or divergence is relatively modest and no literature reviews have ever been made. As in the USA, more recent studies tend to focus on time series (change estimates) rather than on estimated numbers of crimes (level estimates). In Europe relatively more attention has over the years been devoted to analysing convergence or divergence between victimisation rates and measures of fear of crime. Another European preoccupation has been the comparison of victimisation rates across cities, provinces or countries, *e.g.* between the North and South of Germany or the West and the East (Wetzels, Pfeiffer, 1996; Obergfell-Fuchs, this volume). To facilitate international comparisons, a European group of crime researchers launched in 1987 the International Crime Victims Survey which is now in its sixth round (Van Dijk, Mayhew, Killias, 1990). The time series of the ICVS allow analyses of the changes in the ranking of European countries according to the level of victimisation (Van Dijk, Van Kesteren, Smit, 2007). This comparative analysis has repeatedly stirred up debates in the media, especially in countries at the top of the ranking for certain crime types such as the United Kingdom, Australia, New Zealand, The Netherlands, Ireland and Iceland (Van Dijk, 2007a).

In the CRIMPREV study presented here scholars from France, Germany, Italy, The Netherlands, Switzerland and the United Kingdom have tried to compare results of national crime victimisation surveys with national police figures over a time span of two or more decades. This collective effort usefully fills a gap in the existing European knowledge on crime statistics. It allows a revisiting of the some of the conclusions drawn in the extensive American literature from a European perspective. The conduct of such analysis in six different countries with highly divergent national systems of police figures and victimisation surveys adds a unique comparative dimension. To further broaden our analysis we will also draw upon the (European) results of the ICVS. In this report we will try to arrive at evidence-based conclusions on the relative strengths and weaknesses of the two statistical sources. We will also suggest some possible policy implications for the development of a system of (uniform) crime statistics within the European Union.

II. Comparing official and survey-based level estimates for six European countries

Italy has twice participated in the International Crime Victims Survey and a national survey has recently been launched by the Statistical Office (ISTAT) that is now being repeated for the third time (Muratore, Tagliacozzo, 2004). According to the CRIMPREV report on Italy, no work has yet been done on comparing survey-based data with police figures at either national or local level. One reason for this lack of interest is that national police statistics collected by the Ministry of the Interior were till recently paper-based and have recently been fundamentally overhauled, compromising the comparability of police figures over time. The Italian national report outlines some of the other conceptual problems of comparing survey results with police figures such as the problem that police figures only reflect crimes committed and reported within a given territory and omit victimisations that have taken place elsewhere.

In Germany, victimisation surveys at the national level have only been executed a few times and most relevant literature is based on one-off, local surveys. Local crime surveys have mainly been conducted for purely academic interests or to support local crime prevention policies. Researchers have, *inter alia*, examined differential trends in the old and new *Länder* after the unification with East Germany (Wetzels, Pfeiffer, 1996) or levels of crime in the North and South (Kury, Obergfell-Fuchs, Würger, 1995). Innovative work has been done on multilevel analyses of differential victimisation risks of population groups with the use of police figures or other aggregate crime statistics as contextual information (Oberwittler, 2003). The Max Planck Institute for Foreign and International Criminal Law has been partner in two rounds of the ICVS (Kury, 1991). Their analytical work on the ICVS has focussed on methodological issues and on correlates of fear of crime and punitiveness rather than on trends in crime (Kühnrich, Kania, 2005).

The German national report nevertheless lists no less than 34 national or local studies wherein survey-based data have been compared with data from other sources. The results showed that survey-based estimates were universally higher than police figures with 'dark numbers' being more pronounced for less serious (violent) crimes than for property crimes (*e.g.* Stephan, 1976). The apparent reasons for this difference are higher reporting and recording rates of property crimes for reasons of insurance. Many studies have also found that officially recorded crimes tend to be significantly lower than the estimated numbers of incidents reported to the police according to surveys.

In France, The Netherlands, the United Kingdom and Switzerland several studies have been carried out on concurrence between level estimates according to both sources both locally and nationally. Results confirm that such comparisons are indeed far from straightforward. Many cumbersome, and sometimes somewhat imaginative, adjustments had to be made of both categories of data to arrive at roughly comparable datasets[2]. The national reports consistently show that for almost all types of crime, estimates of the numbers of crimes committed according to victimisation surveys are significantly higher than those recorded by the police. This result forms an empirical confirmation of the traditional criminological assumption about the existence of huge 'dark numbers'. They also show that in most cases even the estimated numbers of crimes reported to the police by victims are consistently and significantly higher than the police figures. The latter findings were also found in Germany. It suggest that in all five countries police forces, regardless of legal systems and instructions in place, apply a wide range of discretion in their decisions whether or not to make an official notification of citizen's reports and include it in the official count of crime. As in Germany, the comparisons of level estimates are less divergent for serious property crimes such as car theft or household burglary than for crimes of violence. Together, the results lead to the conclusion that in Europe, as in the USA, official counts of crime consistently and seriously underestimate the true volume of crime and that *de facto* discretion in recording reports leaves ample scope for political manipulation of police figures.

In the French national report the observation is made that proven divergences between survey-based estimates and police figures should be an impetus for police forces to revisit their discretion in processing or not processing victim reports. Police forces should be requested to become more transparent about the screening or 'pruning' of citizen's reports of committed offences. At the same time, the reports also comment on the many limitations of survey estimates. The list of limitations and sources of possible error in these estimates is long. Surveys among households omit victimisations of minors, businesses and of tourists and other non-residents. Homicides cannot be measured other than by asking respondents about family members who may have been murdered. Due to their modest sample sizes, the surveys have limited potential to measure other rare, serious crimes including aggravated assault and rape. They also

2. For example, national police data from Switzerland are only available in very broad categories. Whenever necessary, data were weighted according to Zurich police statistics – which provide a more detailed presentation of offences – in order to produce an adjusted national police incidence rate.

have limited capacity to produce estimates of complex or victimless crimes such as trafficking in illegal products and services and grand corruption. Surveys furthermore struggle with measuring correctly multiple or serial victimisations, especially those committed by intimates. Numerous studies have also shown the tendency of crime victimisation surveys to undercount the prevalence of violence in a domestic setting (Lynch, Addington, 2007). Finally, victimisation surveys suffer, as said, from measurement problems inherent in all survey research such as memory decay of respondents asked to report on past events, forward time telescoping, and biases in sampling designs and in net samples due to non-response. All survey results, finally, are, of course, subject to statistical sampling error[3].

With the exception of forward time-telescoping and statistical sampling error, limitations and proven sources of error tend to systematically deflate rather than inflate the estimated numbers of actual crimes. Victimisation surveys can therefore be said to possess their own 'dark numbers'. The initial claim that surveys can provide a measure of the true size and nature of the crime problem has proven to be untenable. With the current understanding, it seems more realistic, as stated in the German report, to conceive victimisation surveys and police figures as measures of different types of criminality that can complement each other. They should no longer be regarded as competing measures of the same phenomenon.

The emerging consensus among the experts participating in the seminar in Barcelona was that surveys are better at assessing the level of stereotypic volume crimes that are comparatively poorly reported to or recorded by the police. This category includes petty thefts, including pickpocketing and non-motor vehicle theft, burglaries, non-commercial robberies, acts of vandalism and assaults between strangers. Levels of motor vehicle theft can probably be measured relatively well by both systems and can therefore be used for the purpose of cross-validation of the surveys (Lynch, Addington, 2007)[4]. According to the French experience population surveys provide a more comprehensive picture of drugs use among the general population. However, such surveys possess their own biases by not including homeless and other marginalised groups. Police-based data on drugs offences committed among marginalised groups can complement the survey data in this respect.

3. In England/Wales the comparison between the two series is further complicated by the difference in reference periods. Since the redesigned national victimisation survey started to apply a rolling reference period, annual rates have to be constructed.
4. However, also here concurrence cannot be taken for granted. The two series of French statistics on car theft/theft from cars showed significant divergence, probably due to unstable recording by the police (Zauberman, Robert *et al.*, 2009).

In all countries police-based systems seem better placed for measuring very serious crimes of violence such as homicides. None of the two systems seems capable to furnish reliable estimates of acts of violence in a domestic setting. For the measurement of this, politically important, category of crime dedicated studies using special modes of data collection seem called for (Johnson, Ollus, Nevala, 2007)

III. Country comparisons of the level of crime according to both sources

Cross-national comparisons of crime problems can be used to understand the macro-sources of crime and for the purpose of benchmarking national crime control strategies. For both academic and policy purposes, then, it is important to be able to compare the level of crime across countries or jurisdictions. On the assumption that the size of the dark numbers is roughly similar across countries, it is sometimes believed that statistics of police recorded crime, although underestimating the volume of crime, can yet provide a reliable ranking of countries according to the severity of their crime problems. This assumption provides the justification for ongoing cross-country comparisons of police figures as collected by INTERPOL or UNODC.

The ICVS offers the opportunity to compare levels of crime on the basis of survey-estimates. The project also provides an opportunity to study concurrence between the survey-based ranking and those according to international police figures. The correlation between country ranks in terms of ICVS victimisation rates and police-recorded crime rates has previously been examined for a limited number of Western countries (Van Dijk, Mayhew, Killias, 1990). The authors reported that strong correlations between survey-based rankings and rankings according to police figures were found for car theft but only moderately strong ones for household burglary and robbery. No correlations were found concerning violent crimes, including for sexual crimes. For the categories of property crimes the correlations became significantly stronger if the victimisation rates were corrected for reporting rates. The latter finding was to be expected, since by adjusting for reporting rates one of the major sources of error in the police figures is eliminated.

In a subsequent analysis using data from a broader and less homogeneous group of countries from Europe and North America the convergence between relative positions in victimisation rates and recorded crime rates was found to be weaker (Mayhew, 2003). For example Russia and the

Ukraine featured in the top quartile for victimisation and in the lowest for recorded crime while Finland scored in the top quartile for recorded crime but in the lowest for victimisation. As in the previous study, a higher correspondence was found between recorded crime rates and victimisation rates after adjustments were made for varying reporting rates.

Aebi, Killias and Tavares (2002) analysed the correlation for twelve mainly Western European countries between the 2000 ICVS-based victimisation rates for all crimes with the total police-recorded crime rates of the European Sourcebook project, adjusted for reporting (using ICVS data). Their findings confirm the earlier findings of Van Dijk, Mayhew and Killias (1990) and Mayhew (2003), in the sense that robust correlations were only found after adjustment for differences in reporting. Results thus show that among developed countries, recorded crime rates cannot be reliably used as indicators of the relative level of crime. In order to be used for such comparative purposes recorded crime rates must first be corrected for reporting and ideally, if at all possible, for recording practices of police forces as well.

Howard and Smith (2003) looked at the relationships between police figures of the UN Crime Survey, European Sourcebook and Interpol and between these three official measures of crime and ICVS victimisation rates. Their analysis was once again limited to Europe and North America. Their conclusion was *that official measures of recorded crime are mostly consistent in their depictions of crime rates while official measures and victimisation measures were typically in disagreement.* Their results show that for the groups of countries under study, official measures collected by the UN, the European Sourcebook or Interpol are reasonably consistent amongst themselves but show little or no resemblance to rankings based on crime survey research among the public. They also concluded that analyses of the social correlates of crime showed fundamentally different, even opposing results, depending on the data sources used, thus putting in doubt most of the existing knowledge on the macro-causes of crime based on official crime data.

A further test of the usefulness of recorded crime as measure of the relative level of crime should include data on countries from all regions of the world and not just from Europe and North America. Both the UN crime survey and the ICVS contain a measure for 'total crime'. For 39 countries data is available on the overall ICVS victimisation per 100 respondents in 2000 and the total numbers of crimes per 100,000 recorded by the police in 2002. Figure 1 depicts both the number of recorded crimes per 100,000 inhabitants and the percentage of the public victimised by crime according to the ICVS (Van Dijk, 2007a).

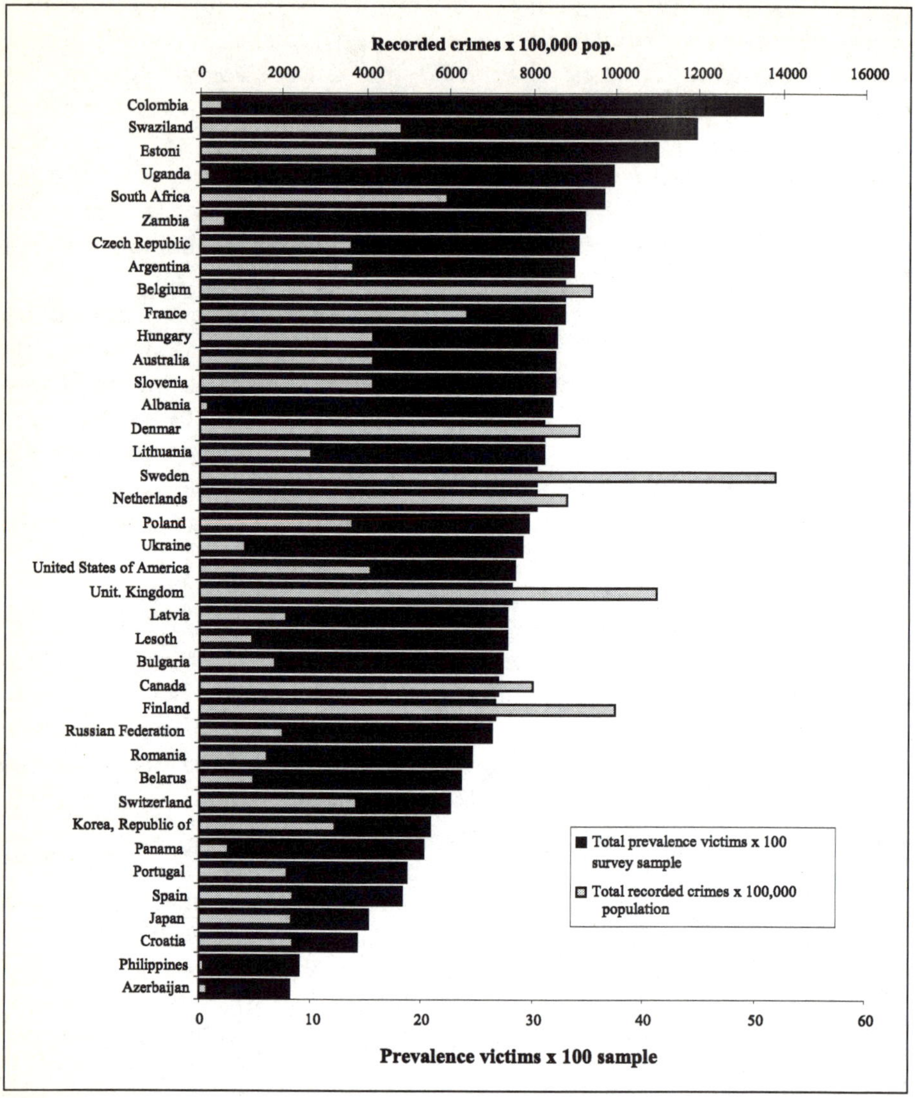

Sources: ICVS 2000 and UN Crime Survey 2002 or latest data available

Figure 1: Total crime, by countries

In the 39 countries with information from both sources, on average 28% of the respondents to the ICVS were victims of at least one crime of those included in the survey. Victimisation rates in the majority of countries (23) were close to the average (between 23 and 33%), while six were well below (Azerbaijan, Philippines, Croatia, Japan, Spain and Portugal) and ten markedly above. Among them, the countries where citizens were most frequently victimised were Colombia, Swaziland, Estonia, Uganda, South

Africa, Zambia and the Czech Republic. In contrast, the highest levels of police-recorded crime were observed in Sweden, United Kingdom, Finland, Belgium, Denmark, Netherlands and Canada, while in Colombia, Uganda and Zambia, which as just mentioned appeared in the group of countries with the highest rates of victimisation, police-recorded levels of crime are comparatively low. It can be observed that four out of six countries with the highest victimisation rates were in Africa, while among the six countries with the highest levels of police-recorded crime five belong to the 15 Member States of the European Union before enlargement.

From a European perspective, it is worth noting that new members of the European Union such as Rumania, Bulgaria and Lithuania show relatively low police figures and moderately high victimisation rates. This finding suggests that dark numbers are comparatively high among new Member States.

The results show that there is absolutely no correlation between the actual level of victimisation by crime and the rates of crime recorded by the police among these 39 countries (r=0.212; n=39; n.s.). Some countries with exceptionally high numbers of recorded crimes also show comparatively high victimisation rates (South Africa) but many others such as Finland, Canada and Switzerland do not. The comparison between country rankings according to ICVS victimisation rates and police recorded crimes was repeated for different types of crime. The results showed positive correlations for robbery (r= 0.663, n=37), and car theft (r=0.353; n=34), while no correlations were found for any other type of crime. An analysis of the correlation between ICVS victimisation rates and police-based crime rates of European countries showed the same results (Gruszczynska, Gruszczynski, 2005).

1. Reporting patterns across the world

One of the strengths of victimisation surveys is that they can give insight in the willingness of citizens to report crimes to their local police. In the case of the ICVS the survey provides comparable estimates of the willingness to report to the police. For ease of comparison, reporting levels were in the ICVS calculated for five offences for which levels of reporting vary across countries and/or experience of victimisation is comparatively high.[5] These offences are thefts from cars, bicycle theft, burglary with

5. Omitted are car and motorcycle thefts (which are usually reported and are relatively uncommon), and robbery (for which numbers per country are small). Also omitted are sexual incidents and assaults/threats. Here, the proportion reported will be influenced by, respectively, the ratio of sexual assaults to offensive sexual behaviour, and assaults to threats.

entry, attempted burglary and thefts of personal property. Table 1 shows reporting percentages for these five types of crime together in 2003/2004.

Country	1989 surveys	1992 surveys	1996 surveys	2000 surveys	2004/2005 surveys
Austria			62		70*
Belgium	60	77		65	68*
Sweden		59	60	61	64*
Switzerland	67		63	58	63
Germany	63				61*
England & Wales	70	69	65	64	61*
Scotland	72		67	62	61
Denmark			.	62	60*
Northern Ireland	44		53	63	59
Netherlands	64	66	58	64	58*
Hungary					58
New Zealand		67			57
France	62		53	51	54*
Japan	.			44	54
Norway	50			.	53
Australia	61	53		53	52
Portugal				38	51*
Ireland					51*
Italy		42			50*
USA	57		58	53	49
Greece					49*
Finland	53	49	53	45	48*
Canada	55	53	52	48	48
Luxembourg					48*
Spain	36				47*
Poland		34	35	43	46
Estonia		33	28	38	43
Iceland					40
Istanbul (Turkey)					38
Bulgaria					35

* Van Dijk, Manchin, van Kesteren & Hideg (2007)

Table 1: Reporting to the police of five types of crime in 2003/04 (percentages) in countries and main cities and results from earlier surveys. 1989 – 2005 ICVS and 2005 EU ICS* (from Van Dijk, Van Kesteren, Smit, 2007)

The results confirm that reporting patterns show considerable inter-country variation.
The highest reporting rates were in Austria (70%), Belgium (68%), Sweden (64%) and Switzerland (63%). With the exception of Hungary, all countries with relatively high rates are among the most affluent of the world. The information on reporting rates confirms that there is a systemic distortion in Euro-wide statistics on recorded crime in the sense that victims in new Member States are less willing to report their victimisations to the police. For this reason alone, it can safely be concluded that dark numbers of crime are larger among the new members than among the old members.
Reporting rates have gone down slightly since 1988 or 1992 in Belgium, Scotland, England & Wales, the Netherlands, France, New Zealand, USA, and Canada, but this is largely caused by the changing composition of the crimes that are reported. Reporting rates have gone up in Poland and Estonia, probably due to post-communist reforms of national police forces that have increased trust among the community. Also in Northern Ireland reporting has gone up since 1988 and 1992 in the aftermath of the peace process.

2. A final test with EU wide data

Within a European context, the hypothesis regarding the universal nature of dark numbers can be put to a test using fresh data from the latest round of police figures of the European Sourcebook (Aebi *et al.*, 2006) and the results of the European component of the fifth round of the ICVS (Van Dijk, Manchin, Van Kesteren, Hideg, 2007). Figure 2 depicts the relationship between overall victimisation rates and numbers of crimes recorded by the police per 100,000 inhabitants.

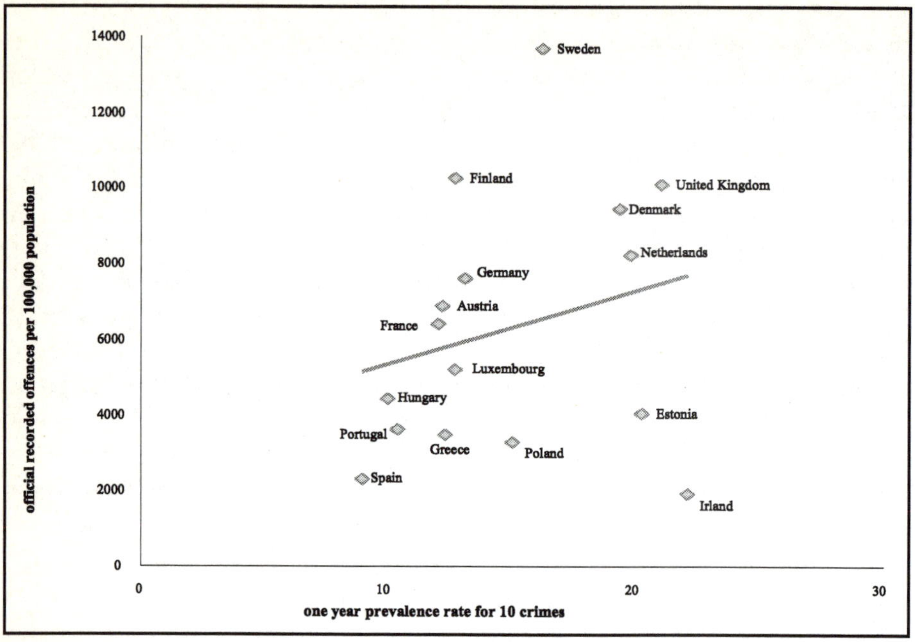

Figure 2: Percentages of victimisation by any crime in 2004 and police recorded crimes per 100,000 population in 2000 in selected EU Member States

Figure 2 shows at a glance that, once again, the number of crimes recorded by the police bears hardly any relationship to the ICVS based measure of crime. The countries with the highest numbers of police recorded crimes are Sweden, Finland, United Kingdom and Denmark. According to the EU/ ICVS, the level of crime, however, is relatively low in Finland and medium to high in Sweden. Countries with the lowest numbers of police-recorded crimes include Estonia and Ireland, both countries with levels of crime significantly above the European mean according to the ICVS. In the cases of Ireland and Estonia the blatant divergence between the two sources is probably caused by deficient recording of crimes by the national police forces. The results confirm our earlier conclusion that police figures are consistently lower among the new Member States of the European Union whereas this is not necessarily the case for rates of victimisation (*e.g.* Estonia).

3. Convergence as correlated rates

Comparisons between survey results and police figures across countries can be made both for the category of total crime but also for specific types of crime. In the latest report on the ICVS, the crime types chosen for a more detailed analysis were motor vehicle theft, theft total, robbery, assault, sexual violence and total contact crimes (Van Dijk, Van Kesteren, Smit, 2007). Although the operationalisations of the offences in the ICVS do not correspond exactly with those used in the Sourcebook for police-recorded crimes (*e.g.* sexual incidents are a broader category than rape), the comparison of the individual types of crime should in theory produce better results than that of overall victimisation with total recorded crime. In order for the police to be able to record a crime experienced by a victim, the victim must have reported his experience to the police. Since reporting rates vary across countries, a better match is to be expected if national victimisation rates are adjusted for differential reporting. Police-recorded crimes were compared with both the victimisation incidence rates and for incidence rates corrected for reporting (incidence rates of reported victimisations). Results are presented in table 2.

Crime type	Incident rates and Recorded		Reported and Recorded	
Motor vehicle theft	0. 48	23	0. 47	22
Theft	0. 39	26	0. 67	25
Robbery	0. 20	27	0. 43	27
Assault	0. 37	26	0. 58	26
Sexual	0. 43	24	0. 54	24
Total contact	0. 27	24	0. 62	24

Sources: 2000 – 2004/05 ICVS, 2005 EU ICS and European Sourcebook 2004

Table 2: Correlations between the ICVS victimisation rates and the recorded crime levels for 7 types of crimes in 2003/04 in 27 industrialised countries

For most types of crime, incidence victimisation rates are only weakly correlated to numbers of police-recorded crimes (*e.g.* 0. 20 for robbery and 0. 37 for assault). The correlations between the two measures of the levels of different types of crime are stronger when victimisation rates are adjusted for reporting to the police, with the exception of motor vehicle theft (a type of crime that is almost always reported). In other words, there is closer correspondence in relative risks of crime when account is taken of differences in reporting to the police. The somewhat stronger correlations found between incidents reported to the police and police-recorded crime indicate that the number of crimes reported by victims is one of the factors determining the officially recorded input of police forces besides the recording practices of the police forces.

In the USA analyst have advocated a correlation coefficient of.80 as a minimum requirement of correlational convergence (McDowall, Loftin, 2007). In the cross-sectional analysis just discussed such coefficient is not found for any crime type, even after adjustment for reporting rates. The comparison of European statistics on police recorded crime with survey-based estimates of the true levels of crime confirms irrefutably that police figures cannot be reliably used to compare levels of crime across EU countries.

IV. Trends in crime over time in five European countries

In recent years, researchers in the USA and Europe have, as said, turned their attention to analysing concurrence between trend data from the two main sources of crime statistics. Even if the absolute numbers show huge gaps, with survey-based data usually indicating much higher levels, trends can still show convergence. Assuming that proportions of dark numbers are constant over time, change estimates from both sources might be similar, even if level estimates are not. Divergence in the trends could point at changes in the production processes of either of the two systems. The identification of such changes can point at the differential strengths and weaknesses of the two systems. We will briefly discuss the findings on trend data from five European countries.

1. Germany

In Germany national surveys have been few and far between. The analysis of concurrence between available trend data from the two systems showed mixed results. In Germany data from three national surveys showed trends roughly similar to those appearing in national police statistics but this did not hold for the new *Länder* in East Germany where reporting and recording seem to have been more variable over time. According to the national report, local surveys in Germany have often indicated trends diverging from those appearing in local police figures.

2. The Netherlands

In the Netherlands survey-estimated crime counts are available since 1975. The initial survey developed by the Research and Documentation Centre of the Ministry of Justice has been implemented by the Central Bureau of Statistics since 1980. The questionnaire used has been a model for many of the surveys conducted in other European countries[6]. The Dutch survey was redesigned in 1980 and in 2004. The available integrated dataset covers the period 1980-2005. According to the data the level of over all crime has remained more or less stable since 1980 according to the national surveys. Police figures show an increase till the mid 1990s. The divergence is most pronounced for crimes of violence and vandalism.

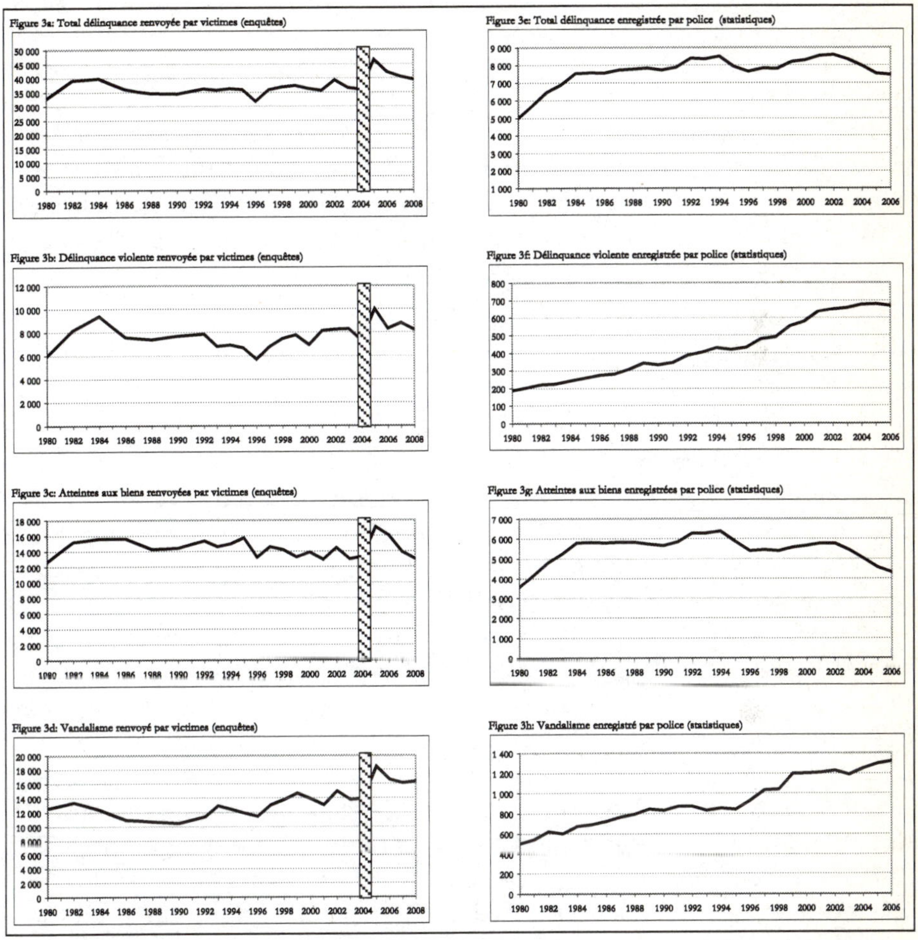

Figure 3: Trends in total crime, violent crime, property rime and vandalism according to police figures and victimisation surveys in the Netherlands 1980-2004 (levels per 100,000)

6. The questionnaire has been a model for the first British National Crime Survey and the Swiss surveys. The Dutch questionnaire has also been the model of the ICVS, launched in 1987. This factor explains the fairly high degree of convergence between both level and the trend estimates from the Dutch and British national surveys and the five rounds of the ICVS (Van Dijk, Van Kesteren, Smit, 2007).

An in depth analysis showed that the upward trend in police figures is largely caused by a lowering of the threshold for recording reported offences by the police. In the Dutch national survey those who have reported an incident to the police are asked whether they have signed an official report. In the Dutch context, it can be assumed that those incidents that have not been recorded in the form of an undersigned certification report will not be officially recorded as offences. The percentage of reporting victims that said to have signed a report has gone up from 60% in the 1980s to 80% in 2004. This increase is largest for violent crimes (from 45% to 60%) and vandalism (from 40% to 75%).
In a secondary analysis of the available Dutch crime statistics between 1980 and 2004, Wittebrood and Nieuwbeerta (2006) proved that almost three quarters of the rise in recorded crime is due to the fact that the police are recording more crimes than before. Only 1 % of the increase is attributable to an increase in actual victimisation risks.

3. England and Wales

In England and Wales detailed analyses have been made of the concurrence between percentage changes of victimisation rates for comparable subsets of offences and police figures over a period of almost three decades (Kershaw, Nicholas, Walker, 2008). The results show estimates for 2007/08 and for previous years in England and Wales, with values for reported, recorded and 'all BCS' indexed to 1981 values as 100%. It also illustrates how reporting and recording rates have varied over time since 1981. In very general terms, reporting rates increased throughout the 1980s and then stabilised. Police recording have fluctuated in different ways at different times. In the early 1990s there is evidence that the police – possibly under political pressure to show falls in crime – reduced their recording rates. From 1998 onwards, a series of policy changes encouraged the police to adopt policies of full recording, which explains the rather erratic recent trends in recorded crime in the five years after 1998. These changes now appear to have bedded in, and recently (since 2004) all three trend lines show a broadly consistent pattern.

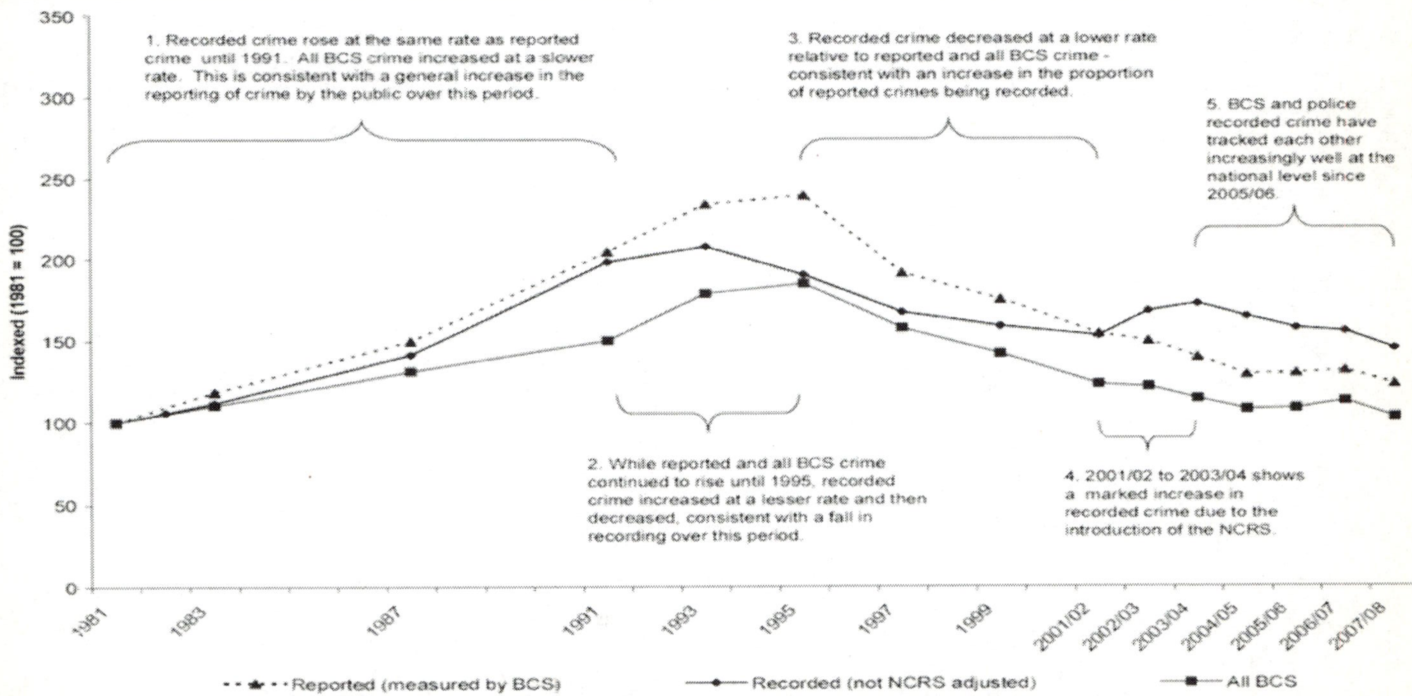

1. BCS estimates of incidents for 1991 to 2007/08 are based on estimates of population and the number of households in England and Wales that have been revised in light of the 2001 Census. For more information please see the Glossary.
2. From 2001/02, reported and all BCS crime relate to interviews carried out in that financial year and incidents experienced in the 12 months prior to interview. Recorded crimes relate to incidents in the 12 months up to the end of September of that financial year. This is so that the recorded crime data are centred on the same period as reported and all BCS crime.
3. To compare BCS and police recorded crime figures it is necessary to limit both to a set of offences that are covered by both series (comparable subset).

Figure 4: Comparing BCS trends with police statistics

What is clear, however, is that, as in The Netherlands, most of the turbulence in the recording process has affected the less serious categories of crime. Figure 4 shows that indexed trends for serious recorded crime largely track the trend for all BCS crime – with the exception of the period in the early 1990s, when recording rates fell even for serious offences. The upward trend in *all* recorded crimes around the turn of the century is largely an artefact of changes in the recording process of less serious offences.

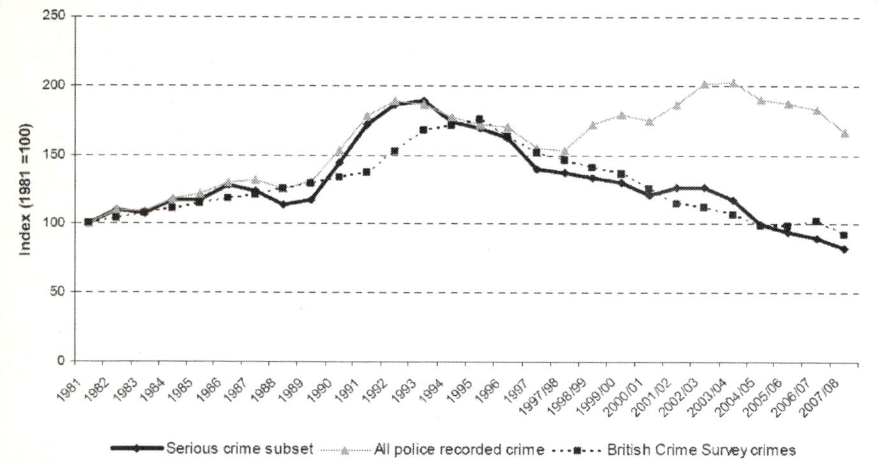

1 The police recorded serious crime subset comprises most serious violence against the person, most serious sexual offences, robbery, burglary, and theft or unauthorised taking of a motor vehicle.

Source: Kershaw, Nicholas, Walker, 2008

Figure 5: Trends in 'All BCS', all recorded crime and a 'serious subset' of recorded crime

4. Switzerland

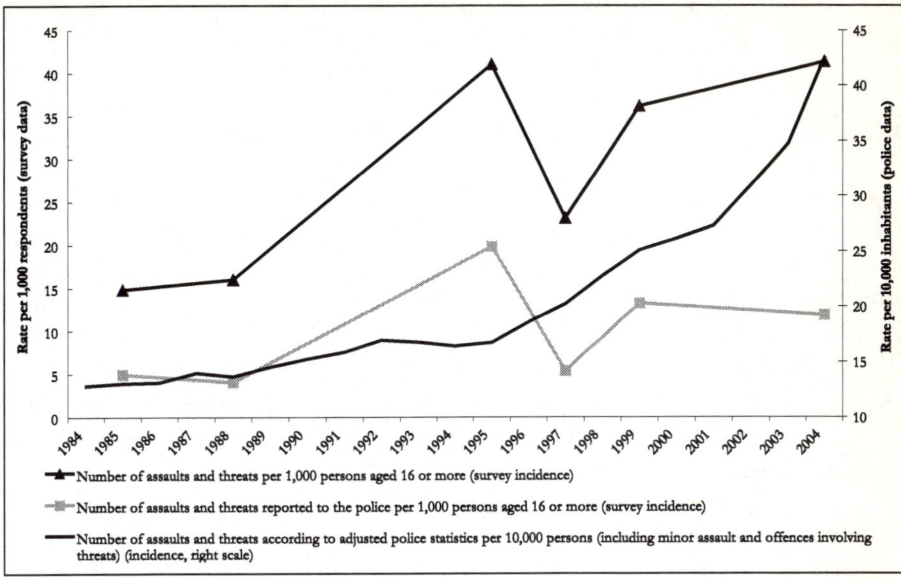

Figure 6: Trends in assault and threats during one year according to the Swiss crime victim surveys and Swiss police statistics

In Switzerland, comparisons between victimisation rates and police figures are especially difficult because uniform crime statistics at the national or federal level are not readily available. Adjusted rates of burglary, non-motor vehicle theft and robbery from the two sources showed remarkable convergence[7]. However, adjusted rates for violent crime show diverging results as is apparent in figure 6.

First, survey-based results on simple assaults show higher numbers not only of actual, but even of reported incidents than the police figures. Second, over the last ten years the level of violent crime has gone up more steeply in police figures than according to survey results on actual or reported crime. The main explanation for these findings given in the national report is that police recording of violent crime used to be deliberately restrained for both legal and policy considerations (including

7. The dramatic drop in the survey rate of theft of motorcycles, mopeds and scooters during the late 1980s, was probably influenced by a change in the law, which made compulsory the wearing of helmets. Police data show a similar trend, though it is less pronounced, possibly because minor incidents often went unrecorded, particularly during the 1980s, when vehicles were often recovered rapidly.

the policy of tolerance for open drugs scenes in Zurich and elsewhere) but has since the mid nineties become stricter. Obviously the explosive growth in recorded violent crime reflects changes in policing rather than in actual violence.

5. France

In France the latest studies of concurrence in the trends of survey-based data and police figures span a period of ten years (1994-2004). The results show several instances of significant divergence (Zauberman, Robert, Névanen, Didier, 2009). As can be seen in figure 7 rates of actual and reported burglary are significantly higher according to the surveys than the official figures. Moreover rates of victimisation by burglary have gone down with almost 50% since 1995 according to national victimisation surveys while police figures have remained constant over a time span of twenty years.

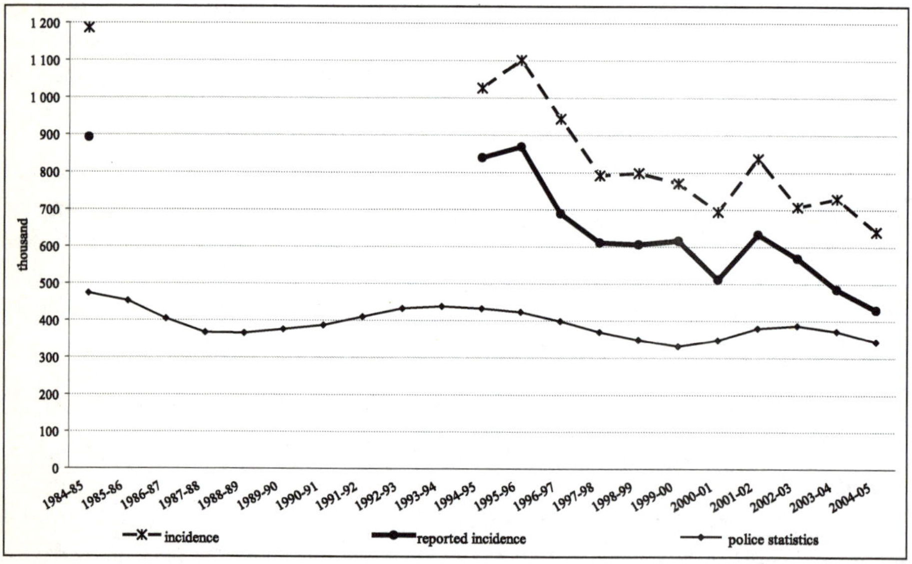

Figure 7: Trends in burglary in France according to survey-based data and police figures, 1984-2005; data from Zauberman, Robert, Névanen, Didier, 2009

The blatant divergence between victimisation rates and police figures on burglary in France over the past decade has been noticed in previous studies (Lagrange *et al.*, 2004). According to the authors, police figures reflect the decreases in rates of victimisation by burglary in a reduced way: *A sort of institutional inertia limits – or at the least retards – the response of*

the administration to an increase or decrease of the raw materials brought to them in the form of victim reports of crime (Zauberman *et al.*, 2009, 38).
The French experience shows several other instances of divergence between the two sources. Petty thefts have declined according to the surveys in recent years but their level remained constant according to the police figures. In the domain of violence, comparisons are complicated by definitional differences. The results show that aggravated assaults have gone up much more significantly according to police statistics than according to crime surveys. According to the authors police figures on aggravated violence have surged as a result of a series of new laws reclassifying more and more types of violence as aggravated assault.

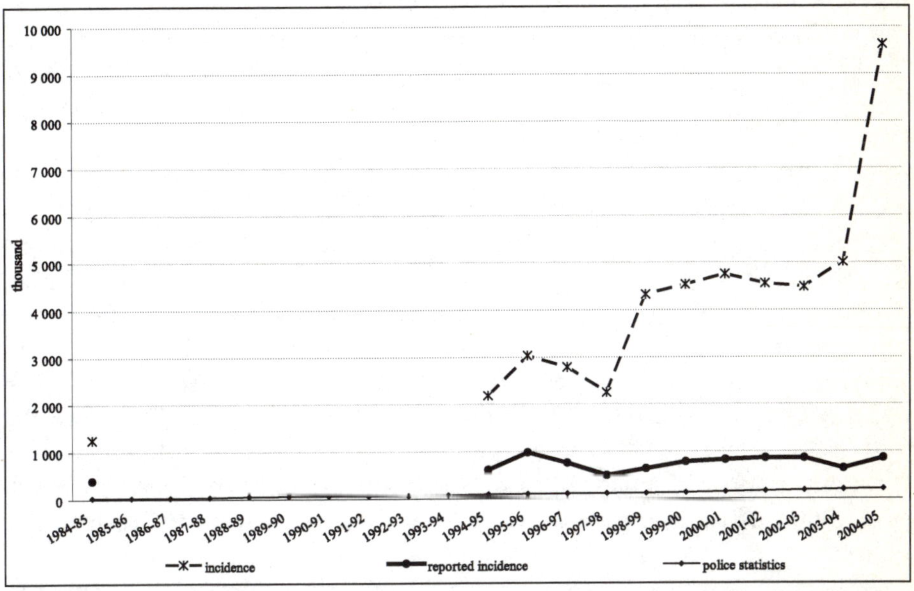

Figure 8: Trends in threats/simple assaults in France according to victimisation surveys and police figures, 1994-2005; data from Zauberman, Robert, Névanen, Didier, 2009

The findings on simple assaults confirm the magnitude of the dark numbers for these types of crime which normally go unreported. In contrast to aggravated assaults, the category of simple assaults shows a significant jump in survey-estimated numbers in recent years which is not reflected in police figures at all.
The divergences between the two sources seem in France somewhat more pronounced than elsewhere. We are inclined to agree with Zauberman *et al.* (2009) that police figures have failed to properly reflect the decreases in property crimes as well as the increase in overall violent crime. The surge

in aggravated assaults seems largely caused by changes in legislation and in recording policies.

6. A summing up

The four countries from which elaborate trend data from both surveys and police administrations are available suggest the following general conclusions regarding concurrence between these two systems. In The Netherlands the stable or declining rates of victimisation by crime have not been adequately reflected in police figures. This is most noticeable the case with petty violence and vandalism. Focussed analyses have demonstrated that the divergence has been caused by improved police recording. In England and Wales police figures seem to have deflated increases in crime in the nineties and to have inflated rates of crime thereafter. As in the Netherlands, the recent spike in violent crime in England and Wales seems largely caused by improved police recording of crimes.

In Switzerland, the police, as in the Netherlands and England and Wales, seem to have improved recording of violent crime in recent years, thereby creating an artificial boom in the official count of violent crime. In France, the two series show divergence in their trends of burglary and petty theft. Stable or decreasing rates of victimisation have not been adequately reflected in police figures, most probably due to better police recording. In France recent increases in petty violence have not been reflected in police figures, as was also the case in England and Wales and Switzerland in the mid 1990s. The recent boom in aggravated violent crime in France seems to be an artefact of changed laws and policies. In this it resembles the surges in violent crime apparent in the Swiss, Dutch and British police figures.

By and large, the results from the four countries indicate that trends in many types of crimes according to the two sources have been divergent due to improvements in police recording of victim reports and, to a lesser extent, increased reporting by victims to the police. The country reports clearly confirm the conclusion that police figures in Europe are highly sensitive to changes in the recording policies and practices of the police and cannot be taken at face value. The hypothesis of stable proportions of 'dark numbers' is unequivocally refuted for these countries in the period under study. The results leave little room of optimism about the capacity of police figures to monitor changes in volume crime over time in other countries.

In the USA several studies have been carried out into the concurrence of trends in survey-estimated counts of crime and police figures since the

launch of the NCVS in 1973. An overview of results is given by McDowall and Loftin (2007). In the USA the surveys have shown significant decreases of victimisations for theft and burglary since the 1980s and for more serious crimes since the 1990s. These decreases are not or only weakly reflected in trends in police figures. As in the four European countries, the main explanation for these divergences is improved reporting by the public and improved recording by the police.
In a focussed analysis Rosenfeld (2007) looked at the divergence between survey-estimated counts of aggravated assaults and comparable police figures. Police-recorded aggravated assault trend upwards during the 1980s and flatten in the 1990s, whereas survey-estimated assaults are flat during the 1980s and decline during the 1990s. Rosenfeld's analysis shows that the upward trend in police figures for aggravated assault results from 'heightened police productivity' in recording such crimes. The conclusions on the analysis of data from the European countries is broadly in line with the general observation of McDowall and Loftin that over the past two decades the measurement of crime by the police has improved while survey-based measurements have remained more or less the same.

7. Other studies

Farrington, Langan and Tonry (2004) compared trends in national victimisation rates with police-recorded crimes of eight Western countries for the period 1980 to 2000. With regard to the similarity between the trends in the two measures over time their results are mixed. For burglary the two trends were significantly correlated for six of the eight countries. For robbery only two countries showed similar trends in police figures as in victimisation rates. Reviewing the available data, Cook and Khmilevska (2005) observed that recorded data and survey results exhibited very different growth rates.
In the framework of reports on the ICVS comparisons have been made between changes in prevalences of victimisation and comparable subsets of police figures for countries that have participated several times in the ICVS. For some countries, comparisons can be made between the trends in ICVS victimisation rates and the trends in total recorded crime. Figure 9 presents the trends of police statistics and ICVS victimisation for total crime in five countries between 1988 and 1999, with observations corresponding to the years covered by the four repetitions of the ICVS (1988, 1991, 1995 and 1999, the calendar year preceding the interviews). Both victimisation rates and police figures are indexed at one hundred for 1988. Taking 1988 as the starting point, the trends on the left and on the right show considerable

symmetry. To a large extent the two trends mirror each other in each country. Crime went up between 1988 and 1991, stabilised or decreased between 1991 and 1995, then further decreased between 1995 and 1999. In the USA the crime drop seems to have started a bit earlier.

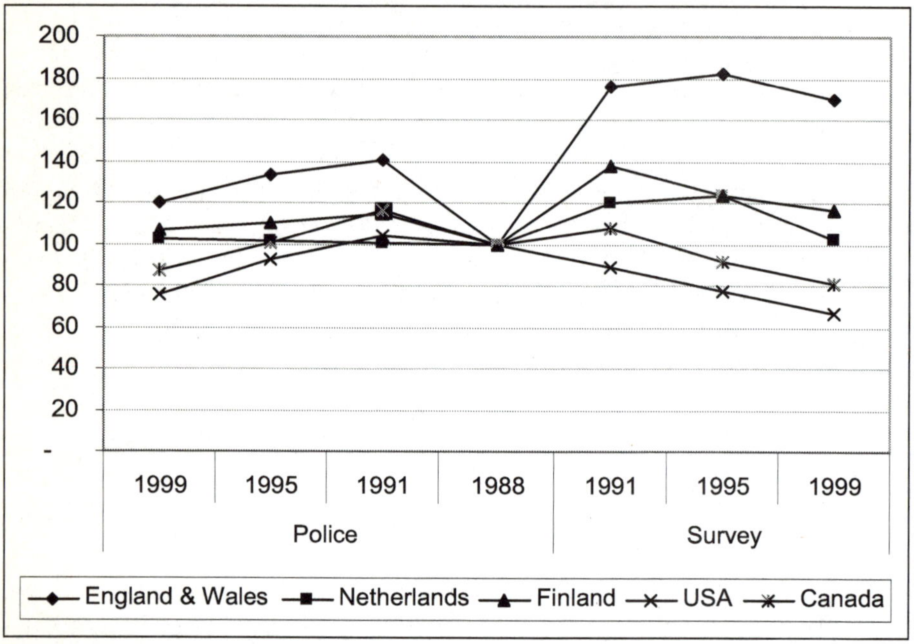

Source: Van Kesteren, Mayhew, Nieuwbeerta, 2000

Figure 9: Police and survey crime trends, five countries 1988-1999 (index 1988=100)

As can be seen in the graph, police-recorded crimes show, as a rule, less marked variation than victimisation rates. The trend analyses indicate that police figures tend to deflate rather than inflate drops in actual crime.

In the USA several analysts have analysed correlational convergence between the trends in NCVS-based rates and UCR figures over the past thirty years (McDowall, Loftin, 2007). Reasonably strong correlation coefficients were found for burglary, robbery and motor vehicle theft but not for any other types of crime. Analyses using survey-estimates corrected for, inter alia, reporting rates tended to show stronger correlations.

In our analyses of the results of the fifth round of the ICVS, we have also looked at congruence between the change estimates during the last few years according to the ICVS and the European Sourcebook (ICVS: 1999-2004; recorded crime: 1999-2003). Comparisons were made between (i) trends in incidence victimisation rates and harmonised police figures; and

(ii) trends in incidence victimisation rates adjusted for reporting and trends in harmonised police figures. Table 3 shows results.

Crime type	Incident rates and Recorded		Reported and Recorded	
Motor vehicle theft	0. 31	14	0. 45	13
Theft	0. 02	14	0. 01	13
Robbery	0. 47	15	0. 50	15
Assault	0. 13	15	0. 06	15
Sexual	-0. 33	15	-0. 35	15
Total contact	0. 17	15	0. 23	15

Table 3: Correlations of trends in crime levels (1999 to 2003 – 2004) and number of countries

The trends in either victimisation or reported victimisation and police recorded crime during a period of 4 to 5 years hardly correlate at all, or, as in the case of sexual crimes, they correlate negatively. Only for motor vehicle theft and robbery weak positive correlations were found. For no single crime type a correlation coefficient of.80 or more was calculated. This negative result is broadly in line with those of Cook & Khmilevska (2005).

The conclusion that trends in crime statistics from two sources are divergent does not by itself suggest that one of the two reflects trends in volume crime better than the other. In England, Stepherd and Sivarajasingam (2005) compared trends in both series with that of a third. They found that decreases in rates of victimisation by violent crime matched decreases according to hospital admissions but differed from the increases in police-recorded violent crimes. Their interpretation of this divergence is that police recording had been improved due to new policing priorities and better technical support (*e.g.* from CCTV's).

This interpretation confirms the conclusions of the national country reports mentioned above. The available evidence suggests that police recorded crime data are too much affected by changes in recording practices to be useful as trend measures of volume crime. To determine trends in actual volume crime, especially also in a comparative perspective, periodically repeated crime victim surveys seem an indispensable tool. To facilitate cross-national comparisons such surveys should ideally be standardised.

We will revert to this issue in the final paragraph.

V. Towards a systemic understanding of divergences between police figures and survey findings

The results of the national reports and of other available studies suggest that police figures, although indispensable for the assessment of homicides and other serious and rare crimes, are unreliable indicators of the level as well as trends in volume crime.

Police figures seem not to be unreliable in a random sort of way. The observation by Zauberman *et al.* (2009) that French police figures seem to reflect changes in actual crime in a deflated or delayed way seems to have general applicability. This phenomenon of 'institutional inertia' has been observed both in the USA and in several other European countries besides France over the past ten or twenty years. This finding suggests the operation of similar forces affecting the production of police figures across the board. The phenomenon of institutional inertia in crime recording calls, in other words, for a further theoretical elaboration.

Criminal justice systems can, within existing budgets and organisational means, respond adequately to only a given number of crimes per year. If more crimes enter the system than can be timely and adequately processed by police, prosecutors, courts or prison departments, the system gets clogged and becomes inefficient. Such system overload generates an institutional need to control the input of new cases. Prosecutors will feel pressed to dismiss less serious cases in order to clean their desks and reduce delays in bringing cases to court (Van Dijk, Steinmetz, 1980). In response to these dismissals police forces will save resources by becoming less pro-active in the detection of volume offences and ignoring citizen's reports of less serious crimes by victims (*e.g.* petty thefts and simple assaults). Such selective recording by the police, whether formalised in guidelines or not, will soon be observed by the public. If victims sense that reports of minor offences are dismissed routinely, they will subsequently refrain from reporting such incidents. They will lift their threshold for reporting crimes to the police.

In our view criminal justice systems effectively exercise control over their input of cases and thereby over their workload. Criminal justice systems do not acknowledge the existence of more crime than what it can properly handle within existing resources. Crime is recorded by the system to the extent that resources permit (Van Dijk, Steinmetz, 1980; Van Dijk, 2007). From this theoretical perspective, the number of police-recorded crimes must primarily be seen as an indicator of the capacity of national law enforcement, prosecution systems and courts systems to process crime cases. Since the available means of police systems and prosecution are generally scarce and determined by factors other than the volume of crime, such as tax revenues, the relationship between police-recorded crimes and the level of crime will always be tenuous at best. More recorded crime reflects availability of more resources rather than more crime.

By the same token police figures are likely to distort changes in levels of crime as well. In years of sudden increases in the number of crimes reported to the police, police administrations and prosecution services will soon be clogged. Reporting victims will have to wait longer, and responsible officers will be inclined to increase thresholds for recording. These processes will in turn discourage victims from reporting. Police figures will therefore often reflect surges in actual crime in a deflated way. Examples are the deflated increases in overall recorded crime in several Western countries depicted in figure 9 in the early 1990s. In contrast, in years of sudden decreases of crimes reported to the police, available human resources will become free for other activities. Such temporary abundance of available resources in police forces can result in improved recording of certain categories of crimes, inviting more reporting of such crimes by victims. Decreases in actual crime will thus partly be offset by better recording and more reporting, resulting in a deflated reflection of the decrease in crime in police statistics of crime.

In the case of the USA and, more recently, France, England and Wales, The Netherlands and Switzerland significant decreases of various forms of crime over the past ten or twenty years seem to have freed resources that have subsequently been used for other purposes. This situation seems to have invited the adoption of new legislation or/and policing priorities to tackle problems of crime perceived to be urgent, notably various forms of violent crime in both public and private domains. This factor seems to have caused increases in police-recorded crimes such as burglaries and aggravated assaults in France and violent crime in England/Wales, The Netherlands and Switzerland. These politico-bureaucratic dynamics can help to explain why the dramatic drops in crime observed in crime surveys in recent years are in many countries not fully reflected in police statistics and why police figures in some countries suggest sudden booms in violence that may not really have occurred.

VI. Conclusions and policy implications

The comparisons between the level of crime according to police figures of recorded crime and results of victimisation surveys in selected European countries, have confirmed that police figures of recorded crime cover only a relatively small part of the victimisations experienced by the public. The size of the dark numbers appears not be constant across countries. Dark numbers seem to be larger among some of the new Member States of the Union. Although levels of victimisation by crime in Central and Eastern Europe no longer differ much from those in the West, the levels of police-recorded crime remain remarkably low (Aebi *et al.*, 2006). For example in 2000, the European countries recorded on average 4,333 crimes per 100,000 people. Most Central and Eastern European countries showed crime rates far below this European average. Results from the ICVS on reporting patterns go some way in explaining this gap. Victims in the new Member States are much less likely to report their experiences as victims to the police, most probably because they have little confidence in the professionalism of the police. Lack of insurance coverage might also contribute to low reporting rates for property crimes in these countries.

The analyses also confirmed that the size of the dark number is highly variable over time. In some European countries divergences between the results of the two systems seem even larger than those observed in the USA. One likely explanation is that both police figures and victimisation surveys in these European countries have been less rigorously standardised than in the USA.

In many European countries victims of crime have over the past twenty years become somewhat more ready to report victimisations to the police. In addition, and more consequentially for the stability of police figures, police forces in some Western European countries have significantly lowered their thresholds for recording less serious crimes. As a result, decreases in actual levels of volume crime are not adequately reflected in police figures of these countries. In some cases recent police figures show dramatic increases in some types of violence which are not grounded in increases of actual violence.

Analysts in the USA have noticed that convergence between the two series has improved during the last decade. Data from the four European countries, notably from The Netherlands and England and Wales, also point to stronger convergence in recent years than before. Police forces in these countries seem to have become somewhat better in recording crimes. Unfortunately, improved crime recording in Western European countries does not improve the prospects for a statistical system of crime information based on police figures in the European Union. Limited availability of resources for the police and the criminal justice system at large and a correspondingly low level of confidence among the public are likely to impact negatively on crime recording in the new Member States. Moreover, our understanding of the production of police figures suggest that if resources for law enforcement and criminal justice and insurance coverage among the new Member States of the EU catch up with those elsewhere in

the Union, police figures of crime in these countries are bound to rise, even when the level of crime may in reality remain stable or decrease.
Compared to police figures from countries with more established police recording systems such as, for example, Scandinavian countries, police figures from many of the new members are comparatively 'unsaturated'. Police figures in the latter countries have the potential to absorb a larger proportion of the 'dark numbers' than is currently the case. Through improved recording and higher trust levels police figures could double or triple without any changes in the numbers of crimes committed. In this respect the stabilisation of police figures in several of the new members should perhaps not even be seen as a positive sign, indicating greater control over crime. This stabilisation could also be a sign of stagnating processes of modernisation and democratisation of the criminal justice systems and law enforcement agencies in these countries. If police forces in the new Member States improve their performance higher divergences between survey-based estimates and police figures are to be expected for some time.
Some authors have argued that police-recorded crime statistics could be used for the measurement of change over time across countries under the assumption that reporting and recording rates remain more or less stable over the years in each country (Bennett, 1991). This assumption is implicitly shared by Eurostat in Luxembourg which has started to release change estimates of police figures from the different Member States and associated countries in its *Statistics in Focus* bulletin (Tavares, Thomas, 2008). In our view, the results of the current study show that the interpretation of past trends in police figures must be carried out with due caution. Trends in European police figures in future years might become even less trustworthy as indicator of changes in the volume of crime.

1. The needs of a standardised victimisation survey for Europe

The EU Action Plan 2006-2010 envisages the development of comparative crime statistics among the Member States including a common module for victimisation surveys. The conclusions of the CRIMPREV workshop underline the need of promoting standardised victimisation surveys in the European Union. The use of police figures of recorded crime for such comparative purposes will almost inevitably result in erroneous conclusions, especially concerning future trends in crime among some of the new Member States. Without a victimisation survey, any comparison between the level and movements of volume crime across the Member States will remain a hazardous, and politically contentious, undertaking.

The single most important objective of the European survey would seem to be to provide an indicator of the relative level of volume crime in the Member States in a comparative, cross-national perspective. More specifically the survey should allow countries to determine how their relative positions change over the years. This would allow national governments as well as the European institutions to benchmark national crime prevention and control policies of Member States and to assess the efficacy of Europe-wide policies.

In many countries the planned standardised European victimisation survey will complement existing, scaled down national surveys such as the ones in France, Italy, the Netherlands, Poland (five repeats of the ICVS), Estonia (four repeats of the ICVS), United Kingdom and Switzerland. Divergences between the level estimates based on the European survey and those of national surveys seem inevitable. Such divergence should be explained to the media as resulting from methodological differences. In the past media have largely ignored divergences in level estimates between national surveys and the ICVS. Media reports have rightly focused on changes in the relative positions of countries according to the ICVS. In our view a European survey should not be marketed as the final answer about crime in the Union but as an approximation of the relative severity of problems of volume crime in each of the Member States.

The questions on victimisation experiences should focus on those offences that surveys can measure best, that is 'stereotypic' volume crime. It seems important to also include a set of standardised and well-tested questions on reporting behaviour and on feelings of safety. Reporting rates are an important indicator of police performance. In many countries criminal policies are set in response to assumptions about fear of crime or lost of trust in institutions rather than to information about levels and trends of actual crime.

Both in the USA and Europe moves have recently been made to scale down the sample sizes and questionnaires of the national victimisation surveys. At the same time initiatives are taken to supplement household surveys on crime with additional vehicles of data gathering in special crime areas (*e.g.* commercial surveys, dedicated surveys on domestic violence and surveys of medical data on violence) (Maxfield, Hough, Mayhew, 2007). For cost reasons a standardised, comparative survey for Europe should preferably be relatively modest in scope and sample size. This feature inevitably limits the capacity of the survey to produce estimates of rarer forms of serious crime but probably enhances its sustainability.

If the European survey is geared towards measuring changes over time in the ranking of countries in terms of crime risks, this argues for an alignment of its methodology, especially its questionnaire, with the one of the ICVS. Such alignment would allow a comparative analysis of trends going back twenty years or more in a majority of Member States. Without such alignment no historical data will be available for trend analyses. Alignment would also preserve the unique option of comparing long term European crime trends with those in the USA, Canada, Australia/New Zealand, Japan and other countries committed to continue participating in the ICVS[8].

2. Complementary information on crime

Although the launch of a standardised European victimisation survey seems indispensable to inform coordinated policies in the domain of crime and justice, this instrument should not be regarded as a sufficient source of comparative crime information in Europe. For a fuller picture of European crime problems survey results must be complemented as a minimum by statistics on police recorded crimes. To complement the survey-estimated data on volume crime, sustained efforts to collect comparative police figures should give special priority to homicides and attempted homicides. Police figures on car theft, burglary and robbery should be collected for monitoring purposes. Comparisons with survey-based estimates of the same types of crime can help to identify changes in police recording productivity.

These core statistics on crime should be complemented by secondary statistics from health institutions on violence, including sexual violence (death certificates and hospital or emergency units' admissions). Periodically, standardised surveys should be carried out about self reported delinquency and drugs use and on crimes against businesses and violence between intimates. Added to these could be assessments from specialised state institutions or non-government organisations of trends in grand corruption, organised crime, financial fraud, money-laundering and human trafficking (Van Dijk, 2007b).

To underline the complementarity of existing crime statistics, they should ideally be presented in an integrated fashion. In the debate at the seminar, it was observed that the production of crime statistics in many countries is occasionally subject to bureaucratic infighting and politically motivated

8. The ICVS was repeated in 2008 in Japan and Estonia. A sixth round of the ICVS, pilot testing new modes of data collection, is planned for the Autumn 2009 in the USA, Canada, Australia, England Wales, The Netherlands, Germany, Denmark and Sweden. Parallel to this, a more extensive draft questionnaire for a European Victimisation Survey will be pilot tested in 17 Member States in the course of 2009 (Aromaa *et al.*, 2007).

manipulation. In the context of international or supranational organisations comparative crime statistics are extraordinarily politically sensitive (Van Dijk, 2007a). In order to promote a favourable reception of a future system of European statistics, comparative statistics should preferably be presented in the form of a comprehensive, annual European Report on Trends in Crime and Justice. Such report should add an explanatory context to the crime trends presented and address topics of cross-national interest. To prevent undue political interference in the preparation of such report, its production should be overseen by an independent board of experts comparable to the one overseeing the work of the European Centre for Drugs Monitoring in Lisbon or the Human Rights Centre in Vienna.

References

AEBI M. F., AROMAA K., AUBUSSON DE CAVARLAY B., BARCLAY G., GRUSZCZYNSKA B., VON HOFER H., HYSI V., JEHLE J.-M., KILLIAS M., SMIT P., TAVARES C., 2006, *European Sourcebook of Crime and Criminal Justice Statistics 2006.* Den Haag, Home Office, Swiss Federal Statistical Office, Cesdip, Boom Juridische uitgevers, Wetenschappelijk Onderzoek- en Documentatiecentrum, [http://www.europeansourcebook.org].

AEBI M. F., KILLIAS M., TAVARES C., 2002, Comparing Crime Rates: The International Crime (Victim) Survey, the European Sourcebook of Crime and Criminal Justice Statistics, and Interpol Statistics, *International Journal of Comparative Criminology,* 2/1, 22–37.

AROMAA K., HEISKANEN M., LAAKSONEN S., VIUKO M., 2007, *Final Report on Crime and Victimisation Surveys*, Helsinki, HEUNI (unpublished).

ALLEN J., RUPAREL C., 2006, *Comparing BCS estimates and police counts of crime*,London: Home Office, [http://www.homeoffice.gov.uk/rds/pdfs06/comparingbcs.pdf].

BENNETT R.R., 1991, Development and Crime: A cross-national time-series analysis of competing models. *Sociological Quartely*, 32, 2, 343-363.

BIDERMAN A.D., LYNCH J.P., 1991, *Understanding crime incidence statistics: Why the UCR diverges from the NCS*, New York, Springer Press.

BUIKHUISEN W., 1975, *Geregistreerde en niet-geregistreerde criminaliteit*, Den Haag: Ministerie van Justitie/WODC.

COOK P. J., KHMILEVSKA N., 2005, Cross-national patterns in crime rates *in* TONRY M., FARRINGTON D. (Eds.), *Crime and Justice,* Vol 33. Chigago, University of Chigago Press.

DIJK J.J.M VAN, 2007a, *The World of Crime; breaking the silence on problems of crime, justice and development across the world,* Thousand Oaks, Sage.

DIJK J.J.M VAN, 2007b, The International Crime Victims Surveys and Complementary Measures of Corruption and Organised Crime, *in* HOUGH M., MAXFIELD M. (Eds.), *Surveying Crime in the 21st Century*, Monsey, Criminal Justice Press, 125-144.

DIJK J.J.M. VAN, STEINMETZ C.H.D., 1980, *The RDC victim surveys 1974-1979*, The Hague, Ministry of Justice. (Research and Documentation Centre).

DIJK J.J.M. VAN, MAYHEW P., KILLIAS M., 1990, *Experiences of crime across the world*, Deventer NL / Boston, Kluwer.

DIJK J.J.M. VAN, MANCHIN R., VAN KESTEREN J., HIDEG G., 2007, *The Burden of Crime in the EU, A Comparative Analysis of the European Survey of Crime and Safety (EUICS 2005)*, Brussels, Gallup-Europe.

DIJK, J.J.M VAN, J. VAN KESTEREN J. SMIT P., 2007, *Criminal Victimisation in an International Perspective; key findings from the 2004-2005 ICVS and EU ICS*, The Hague, Ministry of Justice/WODC, [http://english.wodc.nl/onderzoeksdatabase/icvs-2005-survey.aspx?cp=45&cs=6796].

FARRINGTON D. P., LANGAN P. A., TONRY M., (Eds.), 2004, *Cross-National Studies in Crime and Justice,* Washington, Bureau of Justice Statistics, [http://www.ojp.usdoj.gov/bjs/pub/pdf/cnscj.pdf].

FISELIER J.,1978, *Slachtoffer van Delicten: een onderzoek naar verborgen criminaliteit*, Utrecht, Ars Aequi Libri (diss. University of Nijmegen).

GRUSZCZYNSKA B., GRUSZCZYNSKI M., 2005, Crime in enlarged Europe: Comparison of crime rates and victimisation risks, *Transition Studies Review,* 12, 2, 337-345.

HOWARD G. J., SMITH T. R., 2003, Understanding cross-national variations of crime rates in Europe and North America, *in* AROMAA K., LEPPA S., NEVALA S., OLLUS N. (Eds.), *Crime and criminal justice systems in Europe and North America, 1995-1997*, Helsinki, HEUNI, 23-70, [http://www.heuni.fi/uploads/0gyxd5c8.pdf].

JOHNSON H., OLLUS N., NEVALA S., 2007, *Violence against Women: an International Perspective*, Berlin/Heidelberg, Springer.

KERSHAW C., NICHOLAS S., WALKER A., 2008, *Crime in England and Wales 2007/08. Home Office Statistical Bulletin 07/08.* London, Home Office, [http://www.homeoffice.gov.uk/rds/pdfs08/hosb0708.pdf].

KESTEREN J. VAN, MAYHEW P., NIEUWBEERTA P., 2000, *Criminal Victimisation in Seventeen Industrialised Countries. Key finding from the 2000 International Crime Victims Survey.* The Hague, WODC, Ministry of Justice, [http://english.wodc.nl/onderzoeksdatabase/w00187-criminal-victimisation-in-seventeen-industrialized-countries.aspx?cp=45&cs=6798].

KÜNRICH B. KANIA H., 2005, *Attitudes Towards Punishment in the European Union, Results from the 2005 European Crime Victims Survey with a focus on Germany*, MPI, Freiburg, [http://www.europeansafetyobservatory.eu/doc/Punitiveness.pdf].

KURY H., 1991, Victims of crime – Results of a representative telephone survey of 5,000 citizens of the former Federal Republic of Germany, *in* KAISER G., KURY H., ALBRECHT H.-J. (Eds.), *Victims and criminal justice*, Freiburg, Eigenverlag Max-Planck-Institut für ausländisches und internationales Strafrecht, 50, 265-304.

KURY H., OBERGFELL-FUCHS J., WÜRGER M., 1995, Zur Regionalverteilung der Kriminalität in Deutschland: Ergebnisse des International Crime Survey und der Deutsch-Deutschen Opferstudie, *Kriminalistik*, 49, 12, 769-778.

LAGRANGE H., POTTIER M.-L., ZAUBERMAN R., ROBERT PH., 2004, Enquêtes de victimation et statistiques de police: les difficultés d'une comparaison, *Déviance et Société,* 28, 3, 285-316.

LYNCH J.P., ADDINGTON L.A., 2007, *Understanding Crime Statistics; Revisiting the Divergence of the NCVS and UCR*, Cambridge, Cambridge University Press.

MAYHEW P., 2003, Operations of the Criminal Justice System *in* AROMAA K., LEPPA S., NEVALA S., OLLUS N. (Eds.), *Crime and criminal justice systems in Europe and North America, 1995-1997*, Helsinki, HEUNI, 84-149, [http://www.heuni.fi/uploads/0gyxd5c8.pdf].

MAXFIELD M. HOUGH M., MAYHEW P., 2007, Surveying Crime in the 21st Century: Summary and Recommendations, *in* HOUGH M., M. MAXFIELD M. (Eds.), *Surveying Crime in the 21st Century*, Monsey, Criminal Justice Press, 303-316.

MCDOWALL D., LOFTIN C., 2007, What is Convergence and What Do We Know About it? *in* LYNCH J.P., ADDINGTON L. (Eds.), *Understanding Crime Statistics; Revisiting the Divergence of the NCVS and UCR*, Cambridge, Cambridge University Press, 93-121.

MURATORE M.G., TAGLIACOZZO G., 2008, *The Italian National Victimisation Survey in* AROMAA K., HEISKANEN M., *Victimisation Survey in Comparative Prospective*, Heuni, Helsinki, 100-121, [http://www.heuni.fi/uploads/ojyw1estdwh5b.pdf].

OBERWITTLER D., 2003, Stadtstruktur, Freundeskreise und Delinquenz. Eine Mehrebenenanalyse zu sozialökologischen Kontexteffekten auf schwere Jugenddelinquenz *In* OBERWITTLER D., KARSTEDT S. (Hrsg.), *Soziologie der Kriminalität*, Kölner Zeitschrift für Soziologie und Sozialpsychologie, Sonderheft 43, 135-170. Wiesbaden: VS Verlag für Sozialwissenschaften.

ROSENFELD R., 2007, Explaining the Divergence Between UCR and NCVS Aggravated Assault Trends *in* LYNCH J.P., ADDINGTON L. (Eds.),

Understanding Crime Statistics; Revisiting the Divergence of the NCVS and UCR, Cambridge, Cambridge University Press, 251-268.

STEPHAN E., 1976, *Die* Stuttgarter *Opferbefragung*. Wiesbaden, Bundeskriminalamt.

STEPHERD J., SIVARAJASINGAM V., 2005, Injury research explains conflicting violence trends, *Injury Prevention*, 1, 324-325, [http://injuryprevention.bmj.com/cgi/content/extract/11/6/324].

SCHWIND H.-D., AHLBORN W., EGER H. J., JANY U., PUDEL V., WEIß R., 1975, *Dunkelfeldforschung in Göttingen 1973/74*. Wiesbaden, Bundeskriminalamt.

SCHWIND H.-D., AHLBORN W., WEIß R., 1978, *Empirische Kriminalgeographie*, Wiesbaden, Bundeskriminalamt.

SCHWIND H.-D., AHLBORN W., WEIß R., 1989, *Dunkelfeldforschung in Bochum* 1986/87. Wiesbaden, Bundeskriminalamt.

TAVARES C., THOMAS G., 2008, Crime and Criminal Justice, *Statistics in Focus,* 19, Eurostat, [http://epp.eurostat.ec.europa.eu/cache/ITY_OFFPUB/KS-SF-08-019/EN/KS-SF-08-019-EN.PDF].

TONRY M., FARRINGTON D. P. (Ed.), 2005, *Crime and Punishment in Western Countries, 1980–1999*, Chicago/London, University of Chicago Press.

WETZELS P., PFEIFFER C., 1996, Regionale Unterschiede der Kriminalitätsbelastung in Westdeutschland, *Monatsschrift für Kriminologie und Strafrechtsreform*, 79, 6, 386-405.

WITTEBROOD K., JUNGER M., 2002, Trends in violent crime: a comparison between police statistics and victimisation surveys, *Social Indicators Research,* 59, 2, 153-173.

WITTEBROOD K., P. NIEUWBEERTA P., 2006, Een kwart eeuw stijging in geregistreerde criminaliteit: vooral meer registratie en nauwelijks meer criminaliteit, *Tijdschrift voor Criminologie*, 48, 3,. 227-242.

ZAUBERMAN R., 2008a, *Surveys on Victimisation and Insecurity in Europe*, EFUS, [http://www.gern-cnrs.com/gern/fileadmin/documents/CRIMPREV/WP7/WP7_Brochure_n__1/WP7_brochure1_engl.pdf].

ZAUBERMAN R. (dir.), 2008b, *Victimation et insécurité en Europe. Un bilan des enquêtes et de leurs usages*, Paris, L'Harmattan.

ZAUBERMAN R., ROBERT PH., NÉVANEN S., DIDIER E., 2009, L'acteur et la mesure. Le comptage de la délinquance entre données administratives et enquêtes, *Revue française de sociologie,* 50, 1, 31-62.

Comparisons between victimisation or self-reported crime surveys and official statistics in France[1]

Bruno Aubusson de Cavarlay

The general population surveys that include questions on crimes committed or experienced were first conceived so as to correct the bias of institutional statistics. Generating quantitative sets of data from two different sources on the same issue and then exploiting them jointly represents a comparative approach. But in statistics, comparing two measurements requires verifying, as far as possible, the way they have been arrived at. On this score there has been a broad range of approaches, going from hasty and at times inappropriate juxtaposition to scrupulous examination of the determinants of each source and their impact on the results.

In France comparisons that consist of mere juxtaposition of sources are far more frequent then genuine comparative measurements, as is the case with self-reported crimes and school violence that will be dealt with briefly. As for the latter, *i.e.* genuine comparisons, the list is succinct: on one hand comparisons of results drawn from victimisation surveys of the general of population with police statistics, and on the other a comparison of epidemiological surveys on the use of cannabis with data drawn from the police files on transgressors of drug laws[2].

I. Attempts at matching

In France, surveys of self-reported crimes have not been conducted with sufficient regularity and with sufficient scope to justify close matching with police statistics. The use of the latter source for measuring juvenile crime is of dubious value; some authors have been highly critical of the

1. Translation John Atherton, revised by the author and Renée Zauberman.
2. I have left aside voluntary homicide and the traditional comparisons between court or police statistics and statistics on the causes of death which belong rather to the domain of long-term history and would require a painstaking verification of the legal categories.

representativeness of this source yet have nonetheless relied on it to give socio-economic interpretations of long series of offences classed by category and treated as criminal indicators (Bailleau, 2006; Mucchielli, 2004). To justify this approach, a number of these researchers have resorted to the 'hard core' argument – explicitly (Lagrange, 2006) or implicitly (Roché, 2002) – argument according to which the youth who are the most engaged in criminal activities are less likely to escape being identified by the police and thus, at least as far as the more serious offences are concerned, the statistics should remain reliable. But even when a matching of perpetrators by their names is attempted (Lagrange, 2006), the problem is no nearer solution with serious drawbacks concerning the counting units; surveys count the prevalence per physical individual while the police statistics count separately suspects each time they are implicated in a criminal proceeding.

In the case of school violence, techniques of matching have likewise seen only modest developments. Going beyond the customary presentation of the sources concerned (Carra, Faggianelli, 2006, 27-39), it seemed possible to compare the data collected by the Ministry of Education software program SIGNA with that derived from the so-called victimisation and school climate surveys. The foremost researcher in the field seized the occasion to give an idea of the scope of the underrecording characteristic of the administration's survey (Debarbieux, 2004, 2007). In the course of his demonstration, É. Debarbieux noticed that the SIGNA data registered incidence rates, whereas the survey data measured prevalence; but as regards his conclusion (the vast divergence between the two sources) this did not in his eyes constitute a major drawback. Moreover, after drawing attention to this divergence, the author affirmed that *despite their inadequacies, the official statistics on school violence appear to trace the overall trends relatively well, as do the statistics on crime in general*[3]. Without passing judgement, I would point to the fact that this convergence (between the two sources) is expressed sometimes in terms of trends over time (same overall tendency) and geography (same distinctive characteristics by locality) sometimes in terms of the respective numbers within the various categories of acts listed, which the author refers to as *proportional prevalence*. It remains, however, that these scattered elements of comparison have not been systematized; they have been simply utilized in order to reinforce the image of violence in schools, an image based for the most part on independent surveys the pursuit and development of which the author, as one might expect, advocates.

3. Debarbieux, 2007, 116.

II. Methodical comparisons

1. General population victimisation surveys

Published research

Prior to 2005 the nationwide victimisation surveys on the general population concerned only the various categories of thefts and assaults[4]. In a chronological approach, a comparison of their findings with police statistics could thus be conducted only as concerned these types of crimes. In a first attempt, a team (consisting of Philippe Robert, Renée Zauberman, Marie-Lys Pottier later joined by Hughes Lagrange) drawn from the CESDIP (*Centre de Recherches Sociologiques sur le Droit et les Institutions Pénales*) perfected a method to compare the results of two surveys, conducted at an interval of ten years, with police statistics for the same period (Philippe Robert *et al.*, 1999). The procedure was repeated by the same authors five years later (Lagrange *et al.*, 2004) with serialisation rendered possible when the INSEE (*Institut national de la statistique et des études économiques*) made available the results of the victimisation subsection included annually, from 1996 to 2002, in the survey of household living conditions EPCV (*Enquêtes Permanentes sur les Conditions de Vie des Ménages*/Permanent Survey of Household Living Conditions). With the advent of the OND (*Observatoire National de la Délinquance*/ National Crime Observatory) in November of 2003[5] the national victimisation surveys programme began to evolve. For the 2005 and 2006 sweeps, the questions embedded in the INSEE survey were modified. Despite a few breaks in continuity their results have been taken into account for further updating of comparisons between the data derived from victimisation surveys and police statistics (Zauberman *et al.*, 2009).

In the interim period between the development of the comparison method and the 2008 chronological overview, R. Zauberman, Ph. Robert and their CESDIP colleagues conducted local victimisation surveys themselves in the Paris area: first an Île-de-France (Greater Paris Region) survey in 2001 requested by the Regional Council and conducted under the aegis of the IAURIF (*Institut d'Aménagement et d'Urbanisme de la Région Île-de-France*/ Île-de-France Institute for Urban Planning) and then local urban surveys in 2005 commissioned by the FFSU (*Forum Français pour la Sécurité*

4. Only the very first French survey, that of the CESDIP, included other types of offence which were to be partially reintroduced only from 2005 on (see below).
5. The OND is a department within the INHES (*Institut National des Hautes Études sur la Sécurité*/National Institute of Advanced Security Studies) supervised by the Ministry of the Interior.

Urbaine/ French Forum for Urban Safety). In each case they strove to enhance the results by comparisons with the police statistics, employing the same method[6]. The conclusions varied over the same period from one locality to the next, which meant that, within a relatively circumscribed area, they were coming closer to an understanding of the factors responsible for differences between the two sources, factors having to do with the recording procedures of one or several of the police units.

After the publication of the results of the third Ile-de-France survey in 2005, the IAURIF proceeded itself to compare results with police statistics (Heurtel, 2007) providing an overall view of the three observation periods, the fourth survey dating from 2007 having not yet been incorporated into the series. The method of comparison remained the same as for the first CESDIP survey. At the same time moreover the CESDIP published a secondary analysis of the second Île-de-France survey (Fouquet *et al.*, 2006; Névanen *et al.*, 2007) also including a comparison with police sources[7].

The nation-wide comparisons for 1999, 2004 and 2008 were scientific projects initiated as an integral part of a research centre programme. The local comparisons conducted by the CESDIP were in form of contracts; the victimisation surveys themselves were commissioned, financed and monitored by the local communities concerned. No doubt they benefited in addition from the high degree of expertise of the contracting parties[8], and were thus were in a position to avoid the errors of the first official commentators, overly impressed by the divergence between the results of the victimisation surveys and the order of magnitude that administrative statistics had accustomed them to – in particular when the results were imprudently presented in absolute values.

These first official reactions consisted of the publication in February of 2002 by the IHESI (*Institut des Hautes Études de la Sécurité Intérieure* that was to be renamed the INHES, *Institut national des Hautes Études de Sécurité*) of a *real* crime total of 16.8 million incidents, that was set alongside the 3.6 million incidents recorded by administrative statistics. The institute had obtained funding from the Ministry of the Interior for a more extensive victimisation subsection within the INSEE-EPCV survey,

6. Pottier *et al.*, 2002; Zauberman *et al.*, 2006; Robert *et al.*, 2006; Névanen *et al.*, 2006; Didier *et al.*, 2006a, b.
7. With slightly differing results even though the initial data was the same and the method the same… which is a clear indication of the effects of the differing norms adopted by the authors.
8. The IAURIF study (Heurtel, 2007) adopted the CESDIP method without acknowledging it except, it would seem, for certain hypotheses left without explanation (estimation of repeat victimisation for example).

one which included more detailed questions on the types of victimisation. One of the objectives was to thereby facilitate closer comparisons between sources by phrasing the questions in terms that corresponded to the definitions currently used in police statistics. The comparison was subsequently conducted with the utmost care by P. Peretti-Watel (2000) as part of the internal research program of IHESI, but in a context hardly conducive to a serene examination of methodological issues[9].

In its annual report for 2007, the OND announced that – after the first reports for 2005 and 2006 which had adopted a form of presentation classed by source, beginning with the police statistics – it would give a 'synoptic presentation' of the statistical results concerning crime. *By means of the rate of complaints filed, they* [the indicators provided by the victimisation surveys] *provide an evaluation of the number of offences that are not recorded by the police or the gendarmerie in comparison to those that are counted by the official statistics* (OND, 2007, 25). The comparison between the 2007 victimisation survey and police statistics (for incidents dating from 2006) has been sketched out, but only for the various types of theft (Rizk, 2007b). It is therefore not yet a question of chronological comparisons of series derived from different sources. It only indirectly that this serial approach figures in OND publications with a study devoted to the results of police statistics for thefts between 1988 and 2004. A certain number of results taken from the INSEE-EPCV survey (evolution of the rate of complaints filed) were made the most of in order to assert that *what can be observed through the prism of events recorded by the police and the gendarmerie concerns as well completed thefts* (Rizk, 2007a, 2). These sorts of remarks, scattered throughout the OND publications, add up to an implicit criticism of the comparisons established by the CESDIP researchers. The reader is obliged to line up these methodological elements end to end in order to reassemble a view of the whole. In the interests of clarity I will start with the method employed by Robert, Zauberman *et al.*[10], and indicate subsequently how the different elements recently published by the OND can justify further developments of the comparative method.

9. This state of affairs prompted the setting up in July of 2001 of the Caresche-Pandraud parliamentary mission as a preliminary to the creation of an independent observatory of crime estimation. Today the OND is presented as the official implementation of the recommendations figuring in the mission's report. In practice however the independence of this organisation and its means of controlling the quality of police statistics are severely limited.
10. I will be using this abbreviation to designate the research team (whose membership changed over time) that conducted the comparisons for the CESDIP.

Comparison methodology

Comparing the results of two statistical sources dealing with the same subject (in this case crime) requires a close control of the statistical coverage, of the counting units, and the categories adopted by each source. As far as the statistical coverage is concerned, the major drawback stems of course from the police statistics that count only those cases that are brought to their attention. To pass from the figures relative to the offences declared by the victims to those reported to the police, it is only logical to refer to the complaint rate such as can be ascertained from the surveys.

As concerns the units counted, the French police statistics speak of 'recorded offences' which leads us to conclude, in the terminology of the victimisation surveys, that it is incidence rather than prevalence that is being measured.

Finally the breakdown of recorded offences according to their type on the one hand and the elaboration of a questionnaire asking for replies on the various incidents experienced by the respondents on the other, made it necessary to find – for each major category of victimisation and offence – just the right degree of detail or just the right grouping in the hope of thus introducing a greater degree of similarity between the qualitative contents of the two sets of data.

To remain within these parameters, Robert Zauberman *et al.* estimated – for the same time period (the two years covered by each of the victimisation surveys) and for the mainland population aged 15 years or more – the incidence as expressed in absolute values of one type of offence, an estimate based on the declarations of the victims concerning the number of crimes experienced[11]. Applying to this number the complaint rate as estimated by the survey, they obtained an 'apparent incidence'[12] displayed with a 95% confidence interval. An equivalence in terms of the nature of the offence was sought within the police statistics by choosing the category or categories in which the incidents described by the victims were most likely to have been recorded. The accord between the two sources is

11. In the CESDIP publications, the methodological introduction insisted, in a pedagogical vein, on the connection between prevalence rate, incidence rate, and repeat victimisation rate, but the estimation of the incidence rate came directly from the total number of incidents reported in the surveys. This number, in most cases equal to 0 for non-victims, has no upper limit as given in the questionnaire. Robert, Zauberman *et al.* established a cap for each interviewee to avoid having the estimation skewed by a very few extremely high numbers.
12. This term refers of course, in French sociology of crime, to the traditional notion, of apparent crime, but in English the more familiar term for this notion would be 'reported incidence'[translator's note].

expressed by the inclusion of this police data within the confidence interval of the estimation derived from the survey[13].

In their classification according to the type of offence Robert, Zauberman *et al.* adopted in the national comparisons the same groupings as in the victimisation surveys: namely, burglary, theft of/from vehicles, so-called personal theft (supposedly without violence) and violence (including in principle robbery). One of the major difficulties stemmed from the absence of detail in the INSEE survey questionnaires for the period 1995-2004. For the local surveys, the questionnaires drawn up by the CESDIP researchers were more detailed[14]: domestic violence (between intimates) and sexual assaults were distinguished from ordinary assaults, vehicle crime is broken down into car theft, theft from cars, cycle thefts (including bicyles), and for each of these types of theft, distinctions were made according to whether they had been completed or just attempted, and finally destruction or vandalism were included; burglaries were classified by the type of residence and by whether it was an attempted or completed burglary; violent robberies were separately identified (within the violence category). With this degree of detail the comparisons between the survey results and police statistics were on firmer ground. However the setting up these categories has been a process of trial and error; when results derived from the two sources turned out to coincide, this could easily be taken as an indication of which victims' reports the police had chosen to record or not record. This is particularly perceptible when it comes to attempts. By French law, an attempted crime is punished as if it were a completed act. In application of this principle, attempts should figure in police statistics. Yet this is hardly likely to always be the case, although evidence is almost impossible to provide since, excepting cases of homicides, police statistics do not single out these attempts. Given this situation, establishing a comparison entails striking the right balance, one which would render reported incidence and police statistics comparable, and from this, deduce what the latter are likely to have omitted (for example the attempts, most frequently the case) or what they might have counted in addition (for example through modifying the recording category) which is rare but not unheard of.

13. It is worth noting that if one were to apply the significance-test method more rigorously, it would be the police figures (that are non-contingent) that should serve as the centre point for the confidence interval; in this case the test would justify (with a 5% margin of error) the hypothesis of a correspondence of sources when the estimation (which is contingent) exceeds the interval.

14. The CESDIP 1986 national survey was also more detailed but, since they were operating within the framework of their 20-year serialisation, the authors were obliged to bring their categories of crime researched into line with those (less detailed) of the INSEE-EPCV survey.

But this is not the only problem in regard to police figures. To successfully conduct a comparison it is necessary to focus solely on incidents concerning victims who are included in the surveys[15]. In addition to the question of age and the question of belonging or not to an ordinary household, there is the problem of victimisation of a professional nature. Certain items of police statistics refer specifically to this question, whether it be burglary of professional premises, robbery of financial institutions or violence directed against persons invested with public authority. By contrast, other categories of theft concern "ordinary persons" do enter into the survey coverage. Yet in some instances the distinction is not maintained; thus car theft and car vandalising cases never refer to the type of identity of the owner. This cause of inexactitude is hardly ever mentioned by the authors.

Comparisons concerning assault are even riskier, for the police have set limits for their statistics (excluding petty offences, *contraventions* in the French legal nomenclature[16]), limits for which there is no equivalent in surveys. Since the law has frequently modified the legal definition of intentional bodily harm which, with the interplay of aggravating circumstances, is increasingly classed as a *délit*, the rise that has been observed in police statistics appears artificial. The difficulty is no doubt all the greater given the insufficient coverage in the INSEE survey of violence between intimates, and in particular assault by the victim's partner. This deficiency could moreover turn out to be even more glaring given the fact that repeat victimisation is more frequent for assaults by a partner than for other types of assaults – at least if the theoretical pattern of comparison that includes the transition from prevalence to incidence can be applied[17].

15. In the case of local comparisons it is also necessary to verify that the geographical limits of the two sources are the same by using the survey replies that refer to the location of the incident.
16. The exclusion of less serious offences from police statistics is not particular to France (*European Sourcebook*, 2006). This rule, a vestige of the former code of criminal proceedings that prescribed a specific procedure for all petty offences, became problematic with the appearance of a fifth class of petty offences treated by the courts as *délits*, *i.e.* medium rank offences.
17. In the course of their comparisons, Robert, Zauberman *et al.* repeatedly noted that the units counted by police statistics varied from one category of offence to the next but they considered that, for the most part, the principle was in general to count each occurrence as a unit. The recording of marital violence could have proved to be an exception, at least in the past, because for intentional bodily harm the counting unit was the plaintiff (and not simply the victim). So it would only be the moment when the victim's initiative, on occasion repeated several times, led to the filing of a recorded complaint that the case was to be counted (as one unit) in the police statistics.

These methodological problems concerning comparisons are better analysed and in part solved in the local surveys conducted by the CESDIP. The more recent INSEE surveys, commissioned by the OND, incorporated a good number of these improvements concerning the widening of the categories of offences inventoried and taking attempts into account. But in so doing they provoked ruptures in the series; a fact that the OND remarked on in its publications[18]. I will take up here but two of the modifications for which the consequences have been perceptible.

Robberies cause no end of trouble when it comes to comparisons of sources because of the flexibility of their definition, which varies according to the perspective adopted. Estimating their incidence in the victimisation surveys also depends to a great measure on the way the subject is broached in the questionnaire. At the start the INSEE survey included this type of robbery within the violence category, without being certain that this rule was being respected by the respondents, thus making it impossible to evaluate the incidence. By introducing 'theft with violence or menace of violence' (robbery in other words) as an autonomous screening question, by systematically inquiring about attempts, and by calculating the percentage of complaints filed for the two most recent incidents experienced, the 2007 survey arrived at an evaluation of the reported incidence[19] of robbery well above that recorded by the police. The explanation given for the divergence was the difference in definitions; by leaving aside the figures for robberies with threats of violence (but not actual violence) derived from the victims' declarations, a case was made for a relatively satisfactory concordance with the police figures.

Taking up the method employed in the local CESDIP surveys, the OND also added to the national survey questionnaire (from 2005 on) a distinction between the offences that resulted in the filing of a complaint and those that were entered in the police log without formal charges (*main courante*). Yet the 2007 OND annual report did not take into account the difference that this entailed in the way the calculations were to be done[20]. The results presented by Zauberman, Robert *et al.* (2009) indicated a

18. Rizk 2007b, 89-99. In their most recent attempt at comparison Zauberman, Robert *et al.* (2009) did not consider these breaks to be an insurmountable obstacle, at least as far as the 2005 and 2006 surveys were concerned. Yet one can observe a considerable number of variations that can be explained primarily by the change in survey protocols (in particular a lowering of the estimated complaint rate).
19. Rizk 2007b, 83-85. The author of this chapter of the annual report did not employ the term 'apparent incidence', but did speak of data on the attacks experienced which could be compared to the occurrences recorded by the police.
20. The author of this section of the report indicated elsewhere (Rizk, 2007a) that the former INSEE definition provided not the complaint rate but the reporting rate.

substantial drop in the estimated complaint rate for the two most recent surveys that they made use of: as a result their conclusion that there was an increasing convergence between police records and reported incidence for the various types of robbery might well have come above all from a change in the mode of estimating the complaint rate.
Other methodological questions having to do with the accuracy and the significance of the survey results remain in abeyance. Moreover, C. Rizk (2007a), in charge of statistics for the OND, arrived at conclusions concerning these key questions of comparison between survey results and police statistics that, in regard to thefts, differ somewhat from the conclusions reached by the CESDIP team. In tracing the evolution of the recorded incidents in police statistics between 1988 and 2006, he took as his basis the estimate of the reporting rates for 1997 to 2004 (the INSEE survey year always covering the two preceding years) and concluded that they remained stable except perhaps for the "personal" thefts (that marked a slight increase in reporting rate). He concluded then – despite a "warning" intended to dissuade the reader from equating the trend in the recorded incidents with the trend in the phenomenon itself – that the reasons for the variations in the police statistics were be sought elsewhere than in the decision of the victims when it came to filing or not filing a complaint. The point worth making here is that, in order to arrive at this conclusion, C. Rizk introduced the issue of the accuracy (that was very approximate) of the estimated complaint (or reporting) rate that was based on a very low and decreasing sampling... for burglaries or thefts concerning vehicles (which meant a widening confidence interval). To conclude as to the significance of the trend in police statistics by referring only to the non-significance of the estimated variations of the complaint rates between 1997 and 2004 is open to criticism. But, on the other hand, it is correct to take into account the lack of accuracy of the estimated complaint rate given by the surveys and this most probably does limit the significance of the comparisons, at least in the short run[21]. Given the existing variation rates concerning crime that are generally observed from one year to the next it would be unlikely to obtain significant annual differences for the estimated reported incidence. This would be an argument in favour of long-term serial comparisons; but the breaks in the

21. In their calculation of the confidence interval concerning the reported incidence, Robert Zauberman *et al.* (1999) did not take into account the uncertainties regarding the complaint rate (that was necessarily based on a small sampling of the victims) nor did they take into account the uncertainties regarding repeat victimisation. The figure given for reported incidence is thus that of the prevalence (calculated for the totality of the sample). Their later comparisons proceed in the same fashion.

series introduced by the national victimisation survey of 2007 are not going to make the job any easier.

2. Drug users

Since the creation of the OFDT (*Observatoire Français des Drogues et des Toxicomanies*/French Monitoring Centre for Drugs and Drug Addiction) and the expansion of general population surveys on drug use (or inclusion of specific questions on the subject), police data has been considered as a source of information on the penal treatment of this habit rendered criminal by the 1970 Act. Descriptions of drug users arrested by the police figure in the FNAILS (*Fichier National des Auteurs d'Infractions à la Législation sur les Stupéfiants*/National File of Transgressors of Drug Legislation) that is kept by the OCRTIS (*Office Central pour la Répression du Trafic Illicite sur les Stupéfiants*/Central Bureau for the Repression of Illegal Drug Traffic). This data is no longer considered by experts as a viable means of measuring the level of illicit drug consumption.
An in-depth comparison between the two sources was however made by Peretti-Watel, Beck and Legleye (2004) in an article that appeared in an issue of *Déviance et Société* devoted to the comparison of different crime measurements. It was, therefore, a unique scientific inquiry conducted under the auspices the OFDT, of which the authors were members, thus having access to the files of the surveys supervised by this organization. The study, national in scope, was limited to the cannabis users that form the great majority of the self-reported drug users and for whom the survey samples were numerous enough to be cross-tabulated. The authors first focused on the divergence, initially seen as widening from the early 1990s up to 2002, between the survey data and police statistics, the latter appearing to overestimate the increase in cannabis use (multiplied by three as compared to a doubling according to the survey data). The socio-demographic data that was included in the two sources[22] made it possible to point up certain specific characteristics of the drug users arrested as compared to those self-reported users (more young users, more frequently male, more often unemployed or without a profession, living more frequently in the Paris suburbs or in northern France). Moreover, the use of the survey questions, when taken as indicators of the typologies of the

22. The authors of the comparison did not mention the fact that the recording of arrested users in the national file is not systematic; thus for 2006 there were tabulated in the '4001 file' (covering relevant crime recording activity of the police and gendarmerie) 17,034 cases of use-and-dealing and 115,917 cases of use (consumption) compared to, respectively, 9,376 and 93,817 for the FNAIL records.

various groups of drug users, provided a possible explanation of the divergence between survey data and police figures, in terms of the profiles of the users as well as the evolution over time: the survey data indicated that one category of users was *a priori* more exposed to police arrest, in particular because they bought drugs more frequently and tended to consume them in public areas. These users also displayed characteristics that brought them closer to the 'regular customers' of the penal system. This comparison between user profiles – self-reported or arrested – proved beyond doubt the fallaciousness of the hypothesis according to which the police net operates without bias, that is to say operates in a neutral fashion as regards the various categories of users, a conclusion that up to then could only be surmised from a more general familiarity with police operations.

This conclusion however has to be tempered by serious methodological considerations affecting the counting units in the administrative and the survey sources as well as the respective fields covered.

The question of counting units comes up right away because the police statistics are based on arrests. According to the '4001 file' instruction manual, with respect to drug use and use/resale, the counting unit is the user, it being possible for a single individual to be counted several times in the course of a year. For survey results it is the prevalence rate. Thus, as far as their respective evolutions are concerned, the series could come to resemble each other on account of an increase in the frequency of drug consumption for the self-reported users, which all else being held equal, would render it more likely for them to be arrested. The authors of the comparison indicated that they were going to explore this lead, but in practice they have only done so in regard to the interpretation of cross-sectional data. An indication that would support the above hypothesis is that the divergences between the profiles of self-reported users and arrested users diminishes – but does not really disappear – if one takes into account among the self-reported users only those that are classed as 'regular' users. But this differential evolution of the prevalence of 'regular' use is not empirically exploited to measure the degree of the potential matching of the results derived from this sub-group, at least in terms of trends. If the authors do not dwell on the reasons for their reticence concerning this issue, it is simple to guess why: it would be impossible to give a precise evaluation of the conversion of the prevalence rate into an incidence rate solely on the basis of a classification into three or four groups of respondents defined by the frequency of their cannabis use. The notion of incidence is not really applicable here; it would be rather by bringing the police method of measuring closer to the method that is suitable for surveys that a closer comparison between the two sources could be conducted. In particular it would be preferable to adopt, in police statistics, a counting procedure more similar to that used in the surveys by eliminating multiple counting of the same individual in the course of the same reference period (which is what police statistics always end up doing).

As concerns the field covered by each of the two sources the article by Peretti-Watel *et al.* pointed out that each of them is biased. While on one hand the police statistics undercount the category of users whose profile resembles that of the general population (occasional use, with little or no purchasing of the product), the surveys on the other hand do a poor job of covering for example *out-of-school youngsters, absentees, those living in homes without landline telephones, the homeless or those whose life style distances them from home.* Thus the bias of one source is the contrary of that of the other, and the authors end by concluding that *the police source gives an abridged description of a population that is complementary to that habitually covered by the surveys.*

III. A few comments on the use of source comparisons

1. Cannabis users

The comparison conducted by Peretti-Watel *et al.* (2004) came as a complement to research on policing strategies. The comparison has not been attempted since then with more recent figures[23], and in particular there has been no attempt to determine what category of users was involved in the sharp rise in the number of arrests observed in 2004 and 2005. The presentation of the data collected by the OFDT has not taken into account this comparison, nor has it been substantially modified; moreover little reference to police statistics is made in the annual report. As for the OND, the annual report makes scarcely any mention of police data concerning cannabis use: in the 2005 and 2006 reports, the chapter devoted to the OCRTIS refers to results on cannabis use drawn from general population surveys as frequently as it does to statistics coming from police sources; and in the 2007 report, user data derived from the FNAILS is not even cited.

23. In their recent synthesis (Peretti-Watel *et al.*, 2007) the same authors republished their 2004 article without any major changes nor updating of the data used.

2. Victimisation surveys

In the case of local surveys, interest in victimisation surveys is on the rise, as witnessed by the program coordinated by the French Forum for Urban Safety. While for non-specialist commentators and users, measuring the 'dark number' has traditionally been the primary grounds for recourse to victimisation surveys, the comparison of survey results with police statistics does not appear to be of concern to them. Or, more accurately, it is the results regarding the rate of complaints filed – and these results only – that appear pertinent since, in theory at least, they explain the divergence between the two sources[24]. The rest is treated as purely methodological subtleties that are evoked in passing in cases in which the divergence persists even when taking the complaint rate into account[25]. The important thing for this audience is to possess an alternative measuring instrument, one obtained independently of police authorities. This situation could change once local series become available.
On the national level, the situation is not at all similar. It is evident that above and beyond mere technical considerations it is the pertinence of the statistics as gathered by the police that is at stake. Yet, given this situation, it is astonishing to see that the police statistics continue to be collected without any significant changes as if nothing had happened. The impediments when it come to matching up the two sources are more than evident yet, for the moment, all efforts are focused on transforming the national survey (sampling size, definition of offences, taking into account repeat victimisation) as if adapting it to the norms of official statistics would result in the correspondence of the two, an objective considered as mandatory. On the other hand nothing is done to have the administrative statistics provide a more informative description of the victims that actually do come to see the police or the gendarmerie. The only contributions in this area, in particular for violence for which the statistical categories have not changed over the last 35 years, have been obtained either by monographs (Boé, 2007) or by occasional exploitation of administrative files which is a delicate operation (Bonvoisin, Rizk, 2008). This situation has tended to relegate the issue of the reliability of police statistics to the level of a quarrel between experts. Thus the issue of the

24. One of the conclusions derived from these results concerning the complaint rate could be the plea for more frequent recourse to the police. See http://www.ville-gonesse.fr/delia-CMS/article/article_id-2096/topic_id-216/prevention-de-la-delinquance-la-ville-a-l'ecoute-des-gonessiens.html
25. Hence the synthesis of the 2005 local Saint-Denis survey given by Ch. Bellavoine and P. Salou (2007) which concluded that *the police statistics are more or less comparable to the reported incidence as calculated in the survey (reported offences)*.

clear-up rate that is at the heart of the questioning by Matelly and Mouhanna (2007) of the trustworthiness of police sources in general provoked a defensive response orchestrated by the OND (Ocqueteau, 2007). Reference was included on this occasion to the contribution made by a 'new' source (namely victimisation surveys) but there were no direct repercussions concerning the evaluation of the quality of police statistics. It remains, however, an open question whether simply comparing the survey results with administrative statistics can alone serve as a starting point for an accurate evaluation of the latter's quality. In France, whenever the theoretical model reveals that there are divergences, plausible explanations are found by searching for the combination or combinations of offences that can serve to make them disappear. The divergence is then interpreted as the result of the differing assessments by victims and the police as to the legal definition of the event. But this does not constitute definitive proof, any more than does, in the last analysis, a case of strict correspondence between the two sources. A better understanding of the interface between victims and the police institutions would most probably require, in addition, quantitative surveys conducted on this level of the penal system. The comparison between what the victims report (with or without filing a complaint) and what the police and the justice system handle could, as in the case of drug users, then bear on sociological profiles and not simply the number of cases.

References

BAILLEAU F., 2006, Consommation de masse et prédation de masse ? La délinquance des mineurs en France (1972-2002), *in* LÉVY R., MUCCHIELLI L., ZAUBERMAN R. (Dir.), *Crime et insécurité : un demi-siècle de bouleversements. Mélanges pour et avec Philippe Robert*, L'Harmattan, Paris, 2006, 63-89.

BELLAVOINE CH., SALOU P., 2007, Synthèse de l'enquête locale 2005 sur la victimation et l'insécurité à Saint-Denis, *Saint-Denis au fur et à mesure…*, n°49, 10-20.

BOÉ J., 2008, Violences intra-relationnelles, violences dans le cadre professionnel, violences en situation de la vie quotidienne : les trois grandes catégories de violences non crapuleuses. Élaboration d'une typologie des violences physiques non crapuleuses à partir de l'analyse de plus de 1600 procédures de coups et violences volontaires qui ont eu lieu à Paris entre mars et mai 2006, *Grand-Angle*, n°13, OND.

BONVOISIN V., RIZK C., 2008, Plus de 47500 faits de violences volontaires sur femmes majeures par conjoint ou ex-conjoint ont été enregistrés par la police et la gendarmerie en 2007, soit 31 % de plus qu'en 2004, *Grand-Angle*, n°14, OND.

CARRA C., FAGGIANELLI D., 2006, École et violence, *Problèmes Politiques et Sociaux*, n°923, Paris, La Documentation Française.

DEBARBIEUX É., 2004, Les enquêtes de victimation en milieu scolaire : leçons critiques et innovations méthodologiques, *Déviance et Société*, 29, 3, 317-333.

DEBARBIEUX É., 2007, Évolution et mesure de la violence à l'école en France : 1966-2006, in OND, *Rapport annuel 2007 de l'Observatoire national de la délinquance*, 111-122.

DIDIER E., NÉVANEN S., ROBERT PH., ZAUBERMAN R., 2006a, *Enquête locale 2005 sur la victimation et l'insécurité: Aulnay-sous-Bois,* Guyancourt, CESDIP, [http://www.cesdip.fr/IMG/pdf/EDP_no_99.pdf].

DIDIER E., NÉVANEN S., ROBERT PH., ZAUBERMAN R., 2006b, *Enquête locale 2005 sur la victimation et l'insécurité: Gonesse,* Guyancourt, CESDIP, [http://www.cesdip.fr/IMG/pdf/EDP_no_101.pdf].

EUROPEAN SOURCEBOOK OF CRIME AND CRIMINAL JUSTICE STATISTICS -2006, third edition, Den Haag, Boom Juridische Uitgevers, [http://www.europeansourcebook.org/esb3_Full.pdf].

FOUQUET A., LOTODÉ H., NÉVANEN S., ROBERT PH., ZAUBERMAN R., 2006, *Victimation et insécurité en Île-de-France. Analyse de l'enquête IAURIF 2003,* Guyancourt, CESDIP, [http://www.cesdip.fr/IMG/pdf/EDP_no_104-2.pdf].

HEURTEL H., 2007, *Quel est le chiffre noir de la délinquance en Île-de-France ? Comparaison des résultats des enquêtes régionales victimation et insécurité en Île-de-France » avec les chiffres de la délinquance enregistrés par la police et la gendarmerie*, IAURIF, [http://www.iau-idf.fr/fileadmin/Etudes/etude_136/Quel_est_le_chiffre_noir_de_la_delinquance_en_IdF.pdf].

LAGRANGE H., 2001, Crime et conjoncture socio-économique, *Revue Française de Sociologie*, 2001, 42, 1, 57-79.

LAGRANGE H., 2006, Héritages et performances. Essai d'interprétation de l'implication des adolescents dans la délinquance en Île-de-France, *in* LÉVY R., MUCCHIELLI L., ZAUBERMAN R. (Dir.), *Crime et insécurité : un demi-siècle de bouleversements. Mélanges pour et avec Philippe Robert*, L'Harmattan, Paris, 117-146.

LAGRANGE H., POTTIER M.-L., ZAUBERMAN R., ROBERT PH., 2004, Enquêtes de victimation et statistiques de police: les difficultés d'une comparaison, *Déviance et Société,* 28, 3, 285-316.

MUCCHIELLI L., 2004, L'évolution de la délinquance juvénile en France (1980-2000), *Sociétés contemporaines*, 53, 101-134.

NÉVANEN S., DIDIER E., ROBERT PH., ZAUBERMAN R., 2006, *Enquête locale 2005 sur la victimation et l'insécurité: Aubervilliers*, Guyancourt, CESDIP, [http://www.cesdip.fr/IMG/pdf/EDP_no_100.pdf].

NÉVANEN S., DIDIER E., ZAUBERMAN R., ROBERT PH., 2007, Victimations et statistiques policières en Île-de-France, *Questions pénales*, 20, 1, Guyancourt, CESDIP.

OND, 2007, *Rapport annuel 2007 de l'Observatoire national de la délinquance*, INHES/OND, [http://www.inhes.interieur.gouv.fr/Le-rapport-2007-115.html].

OCQUETEAU F., 2007, À propos de l'activité chiffrée des 'performances' d'élucidation des crimes et délits dans les services de police et unités de gendarmerie (juin 1997-juin 2007), *in* OND, *Rapport annuel 2007 de l'Observatoire national de la délinquance*, 259-265.

PERETTI-WATEL P., 2000, *L'enquête de victimation INSEE-IHESI. Première exploitation de l'enquête* 1999, Paris, IHESI.

PERETTI-WATEL P., BECK F., LEGLEYE S., 2004, Usagers interpellés, usagers déclarés: les deux visages du fumeur de cannabis, *Déviance et Société*, 28, 3, 335-352.

PERETTI-WATEL P., BECK F., LEGLEYE S., 2007, *Les usages sociaux des drogues*, Paris, Presses Universitaires de France.

POTTIER M.-L., ROBERT PH., ZAUBERMAN R., 2002, *Victimation et insécurité en Île-de-France : résultat de la première enquête (2001)*, Paris-Guyancourt, IAURIF-CESDIP, [http://www.cesdip.fr/IMG/pdf/EDP_no_92-2.pdf].

RIZK C., 2007a, En 2006, le nombre de vols constatés par habitants se situe à 33,7 pour 1000, soit son niveau le plus bas depuis 1998, OND, *Grand Angle*, n°11. This issue contains a "Zoom sur…" insert entitled Le taux de plainte en matière de vols contre les ménages et les individus, [http://www.inhes.interieur.gouv.fr/fichiers/OND_Grandangle11.pdf].

RIZK C., 2007b, Victimations et sentiment d'insécurité en 2006, in OND, *Rapport annuel 2007 de l'Observatoire national de la délinquance*, 63-101, [http://www.inhes.interieur.gouv.fr/fichiers/OND_rapport2007_06_VictimationEtSentimentInsecurite.pdf].

ROBERT PH., ZAUBERMAN R., NÉVANEN S., DIDIER E., 2006, *Enquête locale 2005 sur la victimation et l'insécurité: Saint-Denis*, Guyancourt, CESDIP, [http://www.cesdip.fr/IMG/pdf/EDP_no_103.pdf].

ROBERT PH., ZAUBERMAN R., POTTIER M.-L., LAGRANGE H., 1999, Mesurer le crime. Entre statistiques de police et enquêtes de victimation, *Revue Française de Sociologie*, 40, 2, 255-294.

ROCHÉ S., 2002, Audition du 6 mars, *Délinquance des mineurs : la République en quête de respect*, Rapport de la commission d'enquête du

Sénat n°340 (2001-2002) de MM. J.-C. CARLE et J.-P. SCHOSTECK, [http://www.senat.fr/rap/r01-340-2/r01-340-23.html#toc21].

ZAUBERMAN R., ROBERT PH., NÉVANEN S., 2006, *Enquête locale 2005 sur la victimation et l'insécurité: Communauté urbaine du Grand Lyon*, Guyancourt, CESDIP, [http://www.cesdip.fr/IMG/pdf/EDP_no_102.pdf].

ZAUBERMAN R., ROBERT PH., NÉVANEN S., DIDIER E., 2009, L'acteur et la mesure: le comptage de la délinquance, *Revue française de sociologie*, 2009, 50, 1, 31-62.

Comparing crime data of different sources: the German situation

Joachim Obergfell-Fuchs

The measurement of crime in Germany is most often accessed by using the police crime statistics (*Polizeiliche Kriminalstatistik*, PKS[1]). These statistics, in the current form, are available since 1953 and were – except from legal changes – subject to only small modifications, so longitudinal comparisons can be performed for meanwhile about 55 years. These statistics are available and are published for Germany in total as well as for each *Land*. Local or regional police statistics are at best partly published in the media shortly after their publication but can be calculated by the particular regional police headquarter. The police statistics cover one year, but an individual criminal case is included only when the file is forwarded to the public prosecutor or the court, that is after the criminal investigation by the police is completed. Generally, police practitioners characterise the German police crime statistics often as a working statistic which shows what kind of cases the police has dealt with during the past year.

This extensive data source is contrasted by more or less sporadic victimisation surveys. As mentioned elsewhere[2], during the last 30 years, many of these self-report surveys on criminal victimisation experiences and/or own delinquency have been carried out on regional levels. Unfortunately, despite manifold demands, continued national surveys with a standard methodology are not available in Germany until now.

After the completion of such a study quite often the question arises whether survey data and aggregated police data model the same situation, in other words to which extent they are comparable. But at the latest since the remarkable book by Biderman and Lynch (1991), it is common sense in criminology that a direct comparison between these two data sources is hardly feasible without considering a series of precautions. In this regard, the most important problems are differences between incidence rates (police statistics) and prevalence rates (surveys) and between particular reference periods.

1. www.bka.de → Berichte und Statistiken, → Kriminalstatistik.
2. Obergfell-Fuchs, 2008.

I. Stocktaking of studies comparing crime survey data with criminal or social statistics

As mentioned above, continued crime surveys are not available in Germany until now, at best on a local or regional level. But during the last 35 years a set of surveys with different territorial scope and different focus on population had been carried out. These studies are listed in the Appendix. Each of them has been analyzed whether a comparison of survey data with police or social statistics has been accomplished. The list of surveys is based on the former report on crime and insecurity surveys in Germany[3].
The table shows that such comparisons are quite frequent, about three quarter of all these studies considered both data sources, only 8 of 34 studies do not comprise such a comparison. One can hardly identify any characteristics of these 8 surveys, they cover national as well as local territorial scopes and they are focused on the general population as well as on specific groups like students or women.
Analyzing the remaining 26 surveys, the vast majority (n=24) took official police statistics into consideration while 8 (additionally) compared survey data with social statistics data. One survey draw comparisons with school data (n° 16[4]), another collected additional data by handing questionnaires to school officials (n° 15).
The last column in table 1 shows different types of comparative analyses. Besides dark figure calculations, structural comparisons between the different data were drawn as well as multilevel analyses. In the following sections, these different approaches are described in more detail.

1. Dark figure calculations

A mere calculation of dark figures based on the comparison of police recorded statistics and survey data was applied in only five local surveys: The studies by Stephan (1976, n° 1), Schwind et al. (1975, n° 2) in Goettingen, Schwind *et al.* (1978, 1989, 2001, n° 3) in Bochum, Plate *et al.* (1985, n° 6) and Kräupl and Ludwig (1993, 2000, Ludwig, Kräupl 2005, n° 13). It is remarkable that all these studies – except the last wave of two different survey series (No 3, 13) – are quite early surveys, carried out at the beginning of the use of this methodology in Germany. Further, it is noticeable that all theses studies have a strict local scope, none of the following national surveys draw such comparisons.

3. Obergfell-Fuchs, 2008.
4. The numbers in brackets refer to the number of the study presented in table 1.

The methods of these studies are largely comparable. The survey results concerning criminal victimisation were extrapolated to the whole community or to a reference value (mostly 1,000 inhabitants) in order to achieve comparability with the police statistics. In the study by Stephan (1976, n° 1) additional dark figures for household victimisations were calculated. Schwind *et al.* (1975, n° 2; 1978; 1989; 2001, n° 3) used a somewhat different calculation modus by comparing those incidents of the survey which were indicated as not reported to the police with officially recorded police data. This discrepancy built the dark figure. In order to check the validity of the comparisons, all crimes indicated as reported by the survey respondents were compared to all recorded crimes by the police. The results of the survey showed a broad range of dark figure relations (*i.e.* N reported in survey/N recorded by police): Survey n° 1: 1/1 (theft from cars) to 117/1 (attempted robbery); n° 2: 7/1 (theft) to 32/1 (fleeing the scene of an accident); n° 3: 1/1 (aggravated theft, 1986) to 8/1 (simple theft, 1986, 1998), n° 6: 1/1 (aggravated theft) to 16/1 (damage to cars) and n° 13: 11/1 (overall crime rate). Looking at these differences the impression may rise that the results are quite arbitrary, but there is some consistency in the results among the studies: Property crimes concerning insurance benefits (*e.g.* theft of cars) show lower dark figures than minor violent crimes (*e.g.* attempted robbery). Some studies (n° 2 and n° 6) calculated more sophisticated dark figure relationships concerning additional information given by both data sources (*e.g.* amount of damage, victim-offender relationship, time of the offence). But often the case numbers became very low and therefore the statistical range of the particular dark figures got large.
In order to test the validity of the comparisons the number of victimisation incidents indicated as reported to the police has been extrapolated to the number of recorded crimes. Quite often the survey numbers exceeded the police statistic numbers by far (*e.g.* n° 1/7-8/1; n° 13/11/1), only Schwind *et al.* (n° 2) mentioned that there were no significant differences. But such discrepancies have to be explained because they point to a contradictoriness of the two data sources. One possibility could be memory effects of the respondents, *e.g.* telescoping effects, other explanations could be erroneous assumptions among the respondents of having reported the crime, social desirability, or failures in the crime statistics. In the end, a satisfactory solution of the problem could not be found and this might have been one important reason why more recent studies did not calculate such dark figure relationships any more.

2. Structural comparisons

Structural comparisons between the results of victim surveys and aggregated statistics are quite common, in 18 of the 26 surveys such comparisons were drawn. In 12 of these 18 studies only police statistics are taken into account, the remaining 6 studies used police statistics as well as aggregated social statistics. But these structural comparisons are far from being homogeneous, they often include a comparison of the hierarchical order of the particular crimes, different developments of crime numbers over the time (as far as survey series are available), or spatial disparities. Furthermore only few of such comparisons comprise statistical analyses or the calculation confidence intervals, so empirical validation of the results is rather seldom.

Hierarchical comparisons

The idea of hierarchical comparisons is to examine the differences in the relative frequency of different crimes between survey data and police statistics. An example is the study by Arning *et al.* (2004, n° 30). Here, the relative number of victimisations according to the survey data was brought into a descending order and compared with the same crimes recorded in the local police statistics. The results, presented in figure 1, showed differences between the two data sources: damage to property and assaults were dominating in the survey while in the police statistics theft and offences against property were most frequent. The interpretation of these results is quite complex, one possibility is that the willingness to report a crime to the police differs from the willingness to report a victimisation in a survey, other possibilities could be a specific recording behaviour of the police, effects of the survey questionnaire itself, etc. Until now, there is no satisfactory solution of this ambiguousness which complicates the interpretation and refers again to the validity of both approaches.

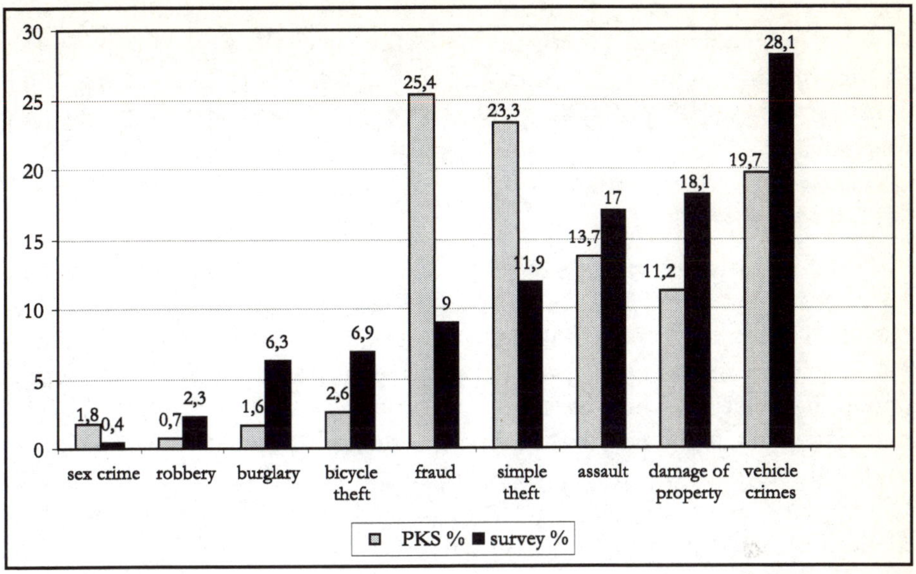

Source: Arning et al. 2004

Figure 1: Hierarchical Comparison between crime statistics (PKS) and survey data

Temporal comparisons

A temporal comparison of the crime development according to police crime statistics and survey results is obviously only possible when there are different waves of surveys with the same or at least a widely comparable methodology. Such comparisons were drawn in five surveys (n° 3, 11, 13, 20, 34). Four of them have a local scope one of them is a national survey. In the national survey (n° 11), Boers (1996) found that the increasing victimisation numbers over the three waves of the survey (1991, 1993, 1995) were equivalent to the increasing numbers of crime in the national police crime statistics. But different trends were found between East and West Germany. These differences were attributed to particular changes in reporting behaviour, but supplemented with the caution that the crime statistics in East Germany are still flawed (Posner 1997, 160f).
The results in the four local/regional surveys were heterogeneous: While Ludwig and Kräupl (2005, n° 13) found a comparable development among both data sources – an increase in crime from 1991/92 to 1995/96, followed by a decrease to 2001/02, with some crimes performing a higher increase in the surveys than in the crime statistics (theft of bicycles, burglary, fraud) – the remaining studies were more skeptical about such similarities. According to Schwind *et al.* (1989, n° 3) the survey results and the crime statistics went in the opposite directions for theft and assault and Baier *et al.* (2006, n° 34) found similar results for violent crimes among juveniles.

They argued that crime statistics and survey data are incompatible because of substantial changes in reporting behaviour over the time which led to a decreasing dark figure. Hermann and Laue (2005, n° 20) stated that such comparisons should only be drawn when long-term developments are available.

Spatial comparisons

Spatial comparisons between survey data and police statistics were drawn by at least 14 studies. Ten of them had a local or regional scope, four were based on national surveys. The main research question of these studies was whether there are similarities in the relative crime numbers of survey data and police statistics among different spatial units. For example do city districts with a high crime load measured in a self-report study also exhibit high numbers of crime in the police statistics? The synopsis of these studies is hampered by the disparate quality and depth of the drawn comparisons. For example in the local studies by Aben (1992, n° 9) or Kury *et al.* (1999, n° 21, Kury *et al.* 1999, n° 22) there was only a juxtaposition of survey results over the analyzed city districts on the one hand and the particular police crime statistics on the other hand without further interpretation and discussion.

Similar comparisons on a local level were drawn for example in the study by Schwind *et al.* (1978, n° 3). They tested a model of constant relationships between dark figures and police statistics among particular city districts. Due to the results the model had to be discarded, not least because the ranges of the dark figures in the districts were quite high. Contrary, other studies, for example by Obergfell-Fuchs (2001, n° 17), found a satisfying match between survey data and police statistics on the city district level: districts with higher crime rates (street crime) in the survey exhibited also higher crime rates in the police statistics. These results are comparable to the study by Arning *et al.* (2004, No 30), they found comparable matches in the relative crime figures among city districts for property crimes and assault however not for burglary, robbery and fraud.

Besides the mere comparison between police statistics and survey data, several studies included aggregated social statistics in order to augment the analyses and the interpretations. Such comparisons are often drawn on a local level, *e.g.* Plate *et al.* (1985, n° 6) found a similar spatial distribution of survey and police recorded crime figures over the analyzed city districts. Especially social stratification in the particular city district provided an explanation of high, or conversely low, criminal burden in both data sources. Similar results were found by Herrmann and Sessar (2007n° 29).

The analysed city district of Hamburg showed comparably high numbers of victimisations, police recorded crimes (PKS) and social liabilities, like high numbers of unemployed, welfare recipients or foreigners. They used the data for modeling unsafe areas. But there were also opposite results, for example Kühnrich (undated, n° 26) showed for the city of Mannheim incoherent relationships between self-report survey data, crime statistics, and social statistics. Besides the problem of comparability of offence definitions in the survey and the police crime statistics, high crime areas (crime in total as well as violent crimes) in the police statistics do not correspond with high crime areas ascertained by the local survey. Likewise, the additional consideration of aggregated social data did not provide consistent relationships with crime load measured by survey data or by police statistics, although in some city districts such coincidences were observable.

Such spatial comparisons are also drawn on a national level. For many years, the national police crime statistics showed that northern German *Länder*, especially Schleswig-Holstein, had a higher crime load than southern *Länder*, especially Bavaria and Baden-Württemberg. In order to validate this discrepancy, additional survey data had been used. For example Wetzels and Pfeiffer (1996, No 14) criticised this "north-south-gap" as an artifact based on disparate reporting behavior of the citizens. According to their study a higher crime load concerning violent crimes was not observable in the north, albeit this part of the country exhibited a higher crime load concerning property crimes in their study too. The authors concluded that the survey data could relativise the results of the police crime statistics. To confirm their conclusion, they analyzed a further survey by Wetzels *et al.* (2001, n° 23). Interestingly these data were not based on a general national survey but on local student surveys in different German cities. Again, they found a higher crime load for victimisations and partially for self-reported delinquency in northern cities than in southern cities. Indeed, these results correspond with the data of the police crime statistics, but the differences in the survey were much smaller than in the crime statistics. They concluded that larger disparities were due to differences in the reporting behaviour between the German *Länder*. They stated a higher willingness to report crimes to the police in the North, while in the South an informal handling would be more frequent.

Similarly, north-south-differences were tested in three other national surveys (n° 8, 10, 18). These results showed a much higher crime load in the northern *Länder* than in the southern *Länder*, therefore national surveys and police crime statistics have the same tendency (Kury, Obergfell-Fuchs 1997). To explain these regional disparities Kury *et al.* (1995) included aggregated social statistics in their analyses (n° 8, 10).

Consistently, the northern *Länder* exhibited a higher socio-economic burden, measured by unemployment rate, economic power, and other social structural variables. Such socio-economic discrepancies were seen as an explanation of the north-south-gap of criminal burden.

3. Multilevel analyses

The structural comparisons described in the above paragraph merely juxtaposed survey data, crime statistics, and social statistics in a more or less sophisticated manner. All conclusions were drawn by simple inspection of similarities or disparities without profound statistical testing. Multilevel analyses offer the opportunity to combine different data levels – individual data and aggregated data. Because such analyses require a more sophisticated methodological knowledge and corresponding special statistical software packages, they are rather seldom. Only three surveys used this method. Interestingly all of them are local or regional, student surveys. In their analysis, Keiling and Funk (1995, n° 16) did not use police crime statistics but aggregated school statistics. They found a considerable correlation between self-reported delinquency (violent crimes and vandalism) and school size, surprisingly in the direction that smaller schools showed higher deviance rates. Enhancing effects on violent behaviour were given by more male and more foreign students in the classrooms.

Oberwittler *et al.* (2001, 2002, n° 25, 27) conducted two different multilevel analyses in comparing different cities and different rural areas. They included self-report data on victimisation and delinquency, police crime statistics and social statistics. The results were heterogeneous concerning the type of analyzed crime (Oberwittler, 2003). A distinct correlation between social burden and criminal burden could be observed for serious crimes (aggravated theft, violent crimes). These, rather seldom offences, were most frequent in high-risk social groups who lived in disadvantaged city districts. Interestingly drug offences occurred more often in less disadvantaged social milieus.

But generally one has to admit that multilevel analyses are to a lesser extent a statistical tool for the comparisons of police crime data and survey data. They can rather be viewed as a promising method for the statistical dealing with data sources of different aggregation levels.

4. Other approaches

In few other studies somewhat different approaches were used in combining survey data with aggregated statistical data. Because these approaches do not perfectly fit into the scheme used above, they are only shortly reported here. For example Boers (1991, n° 7) used survey data as well as police crime statistics in order to describe differences in the assumed possibility of becoming a future crime victim. These subjective assessments correlated higher with the survey data than with the crime statistics. Schwind *et al.* (1995, n° 15) did not use official registered data for the comparisons in their students survey. They additionally asked principals, teachers, caretakers and secretaries to collect official data. These data were compared with the actual survey data. They found that the officials often underestimated violence in schools. Finally, the most recent ICVS (van Dijk *et al.* 2007, n° 33) also compared survey data and police crime statistics. Unfortunately these analyses were only done for the European perspective in total. They found only a weak correlation coefficient between police statistics and ICVS data. In countries with a series of surveys, statistical trends were analysed, again there was an almost meager correlation between the two data sets.

II. Use of the comparisons

Already the author of one of the first German victimisation surveys comparing survey and police data (n° 1) pointed out that a comprehensive comparison between both data sources is flawed (Stephan, 1976). On the basis of his results, he argued that the categories of the police crime statistics and the survey registered crimes are not definitely comparable. While some categories are almost identical, *e.g.* theft of cars, motorcycles or bicycles, others are characterised by a broad range of definition. Most of them are severe crimes like sexual or violent assault. Here the victim's subjective definitions do not necessarily correspond with the legal definitions of the police. Furthermore, on the one hand, the data of the PKS are locally limited and grasp only those crimes which occurred within this well-defined territory, while the surveys also includes victimisation experiences from outside this territory. On the other hand, the PKS includes victimisations of persons who cannot be subjects in corresponding surveys because they live outside the particular territory (*e.g.* tourists). A further point of critics was that the reference periods are

often not directly comparable and that telescoping effects are rather incomputable.
All these problems are well-known for about 30 years of survey methodology and they limit the use of such comparisons. In the first years, there was an euphoric mood that self-report surveys will be able to solve the problem of non-reporting behaviour of victims in order to achieve 'real crime data'. But this perspective and the associated interpretations seemed rather naïve: at that time differences between survey data and police statistics were frequently attributed to erroneous police data and there was a higher faith in self-report data than in the police recording (*e.g.* Schwind *et al.*, 1975). In the following years this optimism has been put into perspective and the opinion grew that both data sources have their distinct errors and that a direct comparison, as for example done with the dark figure calculations (see I.1), bear the risk of multiplying such errors.
These preliminary remarks might be helpful in order to understand the practical use of such comparisons during their (short) history. After the first euphoric idea that it would be easily possible to determine valid dark figures by a comparison of survey data and police statistics, the juxtaposition of police crime statistics and survey data was often used on a *local level* in order to identify high crime areas within in community. In this regard such comparisons were often carried out as part of a local crime prevention scheme (see above I.2) and they allowed the police as well as local public policy makers to substantiate a need for action. Frequently, the results were used for community crime prevention in order to plan target-oriented methods, *e.g.* dealing with high crime areas, ameliorating the confidence in the police, dealing with fear of crime, *etc.* There was a clear relationship between public interest and surveys being part of a crime prevention scheme: similar comparisons drawn independently from these initiatives had more problems being noticed and acknowledged. Comparisons based on community actions were rarely published in detail, they were more often disseminated as unpublished reports for the local authorities (*e.g.* see n° 21, 22, 26, 30). Unfortunately such comparisons often had no time dependent effects, as Kasperzak (2000) showed many results became quite rapidly forgotten.
The use of such comparisons for evaluation purposes has been quite low until now. While the annual police statistics provide an excellent data base for longitudinal comparisons, there is a substantial lack of continuous surveys, also on a local level. These studies can more or less been seen as 'flashlights' and therefore are not appropriate to display a continuous second approach of measuring crimes which would be necessary for evaluation purposes. The scientific use of these local comparisons was also rather limited. While the scientific interest was quite high when the survey

methodology was new, it decreased more and more, mostly because the results were limited just to one community and following studies produced no additional or new findings.

However, this is not the case for all local comparisons. For the multilevel analyses (n° 16, 25, 27) the situation is quite opposite: While they are widely discussed within the scientific community, especially because of their methodology in statistically comparing survey data with aggregated data, their use for public policy makers was more limited. Maybe for the latter group the results were not so surprising and they were less interested in the methodological superiority compared with the mere juxtaposition of results. As a matter of course, according to their scientific relevance such comparisons are published.

With the national comparisons the situation is even more heterogeneous. None of these surveys were primarily intended to compare in depth survey results with crime statistics, therefore the particular studies were more or less a byproduct. Because of the disparity of the German *Länder* and their frequently given competition, public policy makers were in parts interested in these results, especially when election campaigns started[5]. But besides this interest the political use was rather small.

On an administrative level such comparisons had some stronger implications. Since 2001 the German Ministry of the Interior and the German Ministry of Justice publish a periodical security report (*Periodischer Sicherheitsbericht, Bundesministerium des Inneren & Bundesministerium der Justiz* 2001, 2006) where both data sources are considered and at least partly compared. But this comparison highly depends on the availability and the quality of particular studies during the reference period of the report.

Scientific interest and therefore scientific use of the national comparisons is rather moderate, often it was limited to the regional disparities, but unlike the USA there is no German tradition in comparing urban and rural areas across the country. So the discussion is more or less restricted to a small "peer group" and the possibility of relativisation of the police data on the basis of survey results is well-known to criminologists and no matter of an intense discussion.

Finally, some remarks should be made concerning the funding of the comparative studies. Because, as mentioned above, most of these studies were a byproduct of larger surveys, the funding practice do not differ from the practice described in the previous report[6]. Therefore it seems not

5. For example, presentation of regional disparities of crime development to experts of the CDU/CSU *Bundestagsfraktion, Landesgruppe Schleswig-Holstein*, Bonn, 16.1.1996.
6. Obergfell-Fuchs, 2008.

necessary to describe part in detail. The vast majority of all studies were financed by the research institution itself, sometimes as a part of external funding. Concerning the local studies there often was a co-financing between the research institute and local authorities.

*

On all different levels described above similarities and equivalences between police crime statistics and survey data were observable. But there were also remarkable differences between both data sources. These differences cast doubt on the practice of a direct comparison between aggregated police data and individual survey data. For many researchers and especially professionals a simple juxtaposition of the two data sets seemed quite alluring and easy, but the interpretation of the results raises difficulties. But until now it is common practice. Probably this way was and is too simple, both data sources are not simply the two sides of the same coin, they depict different aspects of crime in a particular area.
In a European or international perspective, the lack of continuous (national) victimisation surveys in Germany is quite striking. Often financial limitations are used as an excuse, but for foreign spectators, the situation looks like German authorities were reluctant against such surveys. And indeed, the hurdles for civic participation seem to be quite high in Germany and authorities do even more trust police data than in "vague" polling data. But despite all subjective errors occurring in victimisation surveys, on closer inspection the police crime statistics are flawed too. Therefore the use of both data sources could be a promising way of cross-validation in order to assist a well-balanced criminal policy.

References[7]

ABEN R., 1992, Kriminologische Regionalanalyse Lübeck *in* KOCH K.-F. (Hrsg.), *Kriminalitätslagebilder*, Wiesbaden, Bundeskriminalamt, 305-341 [9].

ARNING D., HIRT M., RENNER F., KURY H. OBERGFELL-FUCHS J., 2004, *Kriminalität und Prävention in Rottweil. Zusammenfassung der Ergebnisse der Bevölkerungsbefragung unter Einbezug polizeilicher Daten und weiterer Kommunen,* Freiburg, unpublished.

ARNOLD H., KORINEK L., 1991, victimisation, attitudes towards crime and related issues: Comparative research results from Hungary *in* KAISER G.,

7. References with a number between brackets at their end refer to the study with the same number in the Appendix.

KURY H., ALBRECHT H.-J. (Eds.), *Victims and criminal justice*, 51, Freiburg, Eigenverlag Max-Planck-Institut für ausländisches und internationales Strafrecht, 99-121 [5].

BAIER D., PFEIFFER C., WINDZIO M. RABOLD S., 2006, *Schülerbefragung 2005: Gewalterfahrungen, Schulabsentismus und Medienkonsum von Kindern und Jugendlichen*, Hannover, Kriminologisches Forschungsinstitut Niedersachsen [34].

BIDERMAN A. D., LYNCH J. P., 1991, *Understanding crime incidence statistics. Why the UCR diverges from the NCS*, New York, Springer.

BOERS K., 1991, *Kriminalitätsfurcht*, Pfaffenweiler, Centaurus-Verlagsgesellschaft [7].

BOERS K., 1996, Sozialer Umbruch und Kriminalität in Deutschland, *Monatsschrift für Kriminologie und Strafrechtsreform*, 79, 5, 314-337.

BOERS K., GUTSCHE G., SESSAR K. (Eds.), 1997, *Sozialer Umbruch und Kriminalität in Deutschland*, Opladen, Westdeutscher Verlag [11].

BUNDESMINISTERIUM DES INNEREN BUNDESMINISTERIUM DER JUSTIZ, 2001, *Erster Periodischer Sicherheitsbericht*, Berlin, Bundesministerium des Inneren, Bundesministerium der Justiz, [http://www.bmj.bund.de/enid/Studien__Untersuchungen_und_Fachbuecher/ss__Periodischer_Sicherheitsbericht_5q.html].

BUNDESMINISTERIUM DES INNEREN BUNDESMINISTERIUM DER JUSTIZ, 2006, *Zweiter Periodischer Sicherheitsbericht. Berlin, Bundesministerium des Inneren, Bundesministerium der Justiz*, [http://www.bmj.bund.de/enid/5396b7ec7d386d744b85270c1f4d76fb,0/Kriminologie/Zweiter_Periodischer_Sicherheitsbericht_der_Bundesregierung_131.html].

BUNDESMINISTERIUM FÜR FAMILIE, SENIOREN, FRAUEN UND JUGEND (Ed.), 2004, *Lebenssituation, Sicherheit und Gesundheit von Frauen in Deutschland*, Berlin, Bundesministerium für Familie, Senioren, Frauen und Jugend [31].

DIJK J. VAN, VAN KESTEREN J., SMIT P., 2007, *Criminal victimisation in international perspective*, Den Haag, Boom Juridische uitgevers [33].

DÖLLING D., FELTES T., HEINZ W., KURY H. (Eds.), 2003, *Kommunale Kriminalprävention – Analysen und Perspektiven*, Holzkirchen, Felix Verlag [17].

DREHER G., KURY H., OBERGFELL-FUCHS J., 2005, Bevölkerungsumfragen in ländlichen und städtischen Regionen – Kriminalitätsanalysen und gezielte proaktive Maßnahmen am Beispiel der Stadt Rottweil *in* BANNENBERG, B., COESTER M., MARKS E. (Hrsg.), *Kommunale Kriminalprävention*, Mönchengladbach, Forum Verlag Godesberg, 169-188 [30].

FELTES T., GOLDBERG B., 2006, Selbstberichtete Delinquenz, Viktimisierung und Verbrechensfurcht bei Schülern mit und ohne Migrationshintergrund *in* OBERGFELL-FUCHS J., BRANDENSTEIN M. (Hrsg.). *Nationale und internationale Entwicklungen in der Kriminologie. Festschrift für Helmut Kury zum 65. Geburtstag*, Frankfurt/Main, Verlag für Polizeiwissenschaft, 203-237 [32].

FORSCHUNGSGRUPPE KOMMUNALE KRIMINALPRÄVENTION IN BADEN-WÜRTTEMBERG, 1998, Viktimisierungen, Kriminalitätsfurcht und Bewertung der Polizei in Deutschland. *Monatsschrift für Kriminologie und Strafrechtsreform*, 81, 2, 67-82 [18].

FUNK W. (Hrsg.), 1995, *Nürnberger Schüler-Studie 1994*, Regensburg, S. Roderer Verlag [16].

HERMANN D. LAUE C., 2005, Wirkungen kommunaler Kriminalprävention – Ein Fallbeispiel *in* BANNENBERG B., COESTER M., MARKS E. (Hrsg.), *Kommunale Kriminalprävention. Ausgewählte Beiträge des 9. Deutschen Präventionstages*, Mönchengladbach, Forum Verlag Godesberg, 197-208 [20].

HERMANN D., DÖLLING D., 2001, *Kriminalprävention und Wertorientierungen in komplexen Gesellschaften*, Mainz, Weisser Ring, [24]

HERRMANN H. SESSAR K., 2007, Zur Kontextualisierung von Unsicherheit und Furcht im urbanen Raum: der Fall Wilhelmsburg/Hamburg *in* SESSAR K., W. STANGL W., VAN SWAANINGEN R., (Hrsg.), *Großstadtängste – Anxious Cities*, Wien, LIT-Verlag, 189-228.

KASPERZAK T., 2000, *Stadtstruktur, Kriminalitätsbelastung und Verbrechensfurcht*, Holzkirchen, Felix Verlag.

KEILING K. FUNK W., 1995, Die Relevanz des Sozialkontextes der Schule für die Gewaltbilligung, Gewaltbereitschaft und Gewalttätigkeit der Nürnberger Schüler *in* FUNK W. (Hrsg.), *Nürnberger Schüler Studie 1994, Gewalt an Schulen*, Regensburg, S. Roderer Verlag, 189-222.

KRÄUPL G. LUDWIG H., 1993, *Wandel kommunaler Lebenslagen, Kriminalität und Sanktionserwartungen. Bevölkerungsbefragung in einer städtischen Region Thüringens1991/92 (Jenaer Kriminalitätsbefragung)*, Freiburg, Eigenverlag Max-Planck-Institut für ausländisches und internationales Strafrecht [13].

KRÄUPL G. LUDWIG H., 2000, *Wahrnehmung von Kriminalität und Sanktionen im Kontext gesellschaftlicher Transformation*, Freiburg, edition iuscrim [13].

KREUZER A., GÖRGEN T., KRÜGER R., MÜNCH V. SCHNEIDER H., 1993, *Jugenddelinquenz in Ost und West*, Bonn, Forum Verlag Godesberg [4].

KÜHNRICH B., KURY H. OBERGFELL-FUCHS J., undated, *Gegenüberstellung soziodemographischer Daten und derkriminologischen Dunkelfeldanalyse der Stadt Mannheim*, Freiburg, unpublished.

KURY H., 1991, Victims of crime – Results of a representative telephone survey of 5,000 citizens of the former Federal Republic of Germany *in* KAISER G., KURY H., ALBRECHT H.-J. [Eds.), *Victims and criminal justice*, 50, Freiburg, Eigenverlag Max-Planck-Institut für ausländisches und internationales Strafrecht, 265-304 [8].

KURY H., DÖRMANN U., RICHTER H., WÜRGER M., 1992, *Opfererfahrungen und Meinungen zur Inneren Sicherheit in Deutschland,* Wiesbaden, Bundeskriminalamt [10].

KURY H., OBERGFELL-FUCHS J., BRAUN V., 1999, *Kriminologische Dunkelfeldanalyse der Stadt Reutlingen*, Freiburg, unpublished [21].

KURY H., OBERGFELL-FUCHS J., TELL S., 1999, *Kriminologische Dunkelfeldanalyse der Stadt Metzingen*, Freiburg, unpublished [22].

KURY H., OBERGFELL-FUCHS J. WÜRGER M., 2000, *Gemeinde und Kriminalität. Eine Untersuchung in Ost- und Westdeutschland*, Freiburg, edition iuscrim [12].

KURY H., OBERGFELL-FUCHS J., 1997, Zur Regionalverteilung von Kriminalität – eine Antwort auf Kritik, *Monatsschrift für Kriminologie und Strafrechtsreform*, 80, 5, 346-351.

KURY H., OBERGFELL-FUCHS J., WÜRGER M., 1995, Zur Regionalverteilung der Kriminalität in Deutschland Ergebnisse des International Crime Survey und der Deutsch-Deutschen Opferstudie, *Kriminalistik*, 49, 12, 769-778.

LUDWIG H., KRÄUPL G., 2005, *Viktimisierung, Sanktionen und Strafverfolgung. Jenaer Kriminalitätsbefragung über ein Jahrzehnt gesellschaftlicher Transformation,* Mönchengladbach, Forum Verlag Godesberg [13].

OBERGFELL FUCHS J., 2001, *Ansätze und Strategien kommunaler Kriminalprävention – Begleitforschung im Pilotprojekt Kommunale Kriminalprävention in Baden-Württemberg anhand der Stadt Freiburg im Breisgau,* Freiburg, edition iuscrim.

OBERGFELL-FUCHS J., 2008, Crime victims and insecurity surveys in Germany *in* ZAUBERMAN R. (Ed.) *Victimisation and Insecurity in Europe. A review of Surveys and Their Use*, Brussels, VUB Press, 105-125.

OBERWITTLER D., 2003, Stadtstruktur, Freundeskreise und Delinquenz. Eine Mehrebenenanalyse zu sozialökologischen Kontexteffekten auf schwere Jugenddelinquenz *in* OBERWITTLER D., KARSTEDT S. (Hrsg.), Soziologie der Kriminalität, *Kölner Zeitschrift für Soziologie und Sozialpsychologie, Sonderheft* 43/2003, Wiesbaden, VS Verlag für Sozialwissenschaften, 135-170.

OBERWITTLER D., BLANK T., KÖLLISCH T., NAPLAVA T., 2001, *Soziale Lebenslagen und Delinquenz von Jugendlichen. Arbeitsberichte 1/2001,*

Freiburg, Max-Planck-Institut für ausländisches und internationales Strafrecht [25].

OBERWITTLER D., KÖLLISCH T., NAPLAVA T., BLANK T., 2002, *MPI-Schulbefragung Breisgau/Markgräfler Land 2000*, Freiburg, Max-Planck-Institut für ausländisches und internationales Strafrecht, [http://www.mpicc.de/shared/data/pdf/workingpaper8.pdf], [27].

PLATE M., SCHWINGES U., WEIß R., 1985, *Strukturen der Kriminalität in Solingen*, Wiesbaden, Bundeskriminalamt [6].

POSCH C., MAIER I., KURY H., OBERGFELL-FUCHS J., 2001, *Kriminologische Dunkelfeldanalyse der Stadt Mannheim*, Freiburg, unpublished [26].

POSNER C., 1997, Die Täterbefragung im Kontext "Sozialer Umbruch und Kriminalität" *in* BOERS K., GUTSCHE G., SESSAR K. (Hrsg.), *Sozialer Umbruch und Kriminalität in Deutschland*, Opladen, Westdeutscher Verlag, 157-185.

SCHNELL R., KREUTER F., 2000, Untersuchungen zur Ursache unterschiedlicher Ergebnisse sehr ähnlicher Viktimisierungssurveys, *Kölner Zeitschrift für Soziologie und Sozialpsychologie*, 52, 1, 96-117 [19].

SCHWIND H.-D., AHLBORN W., EGER H. J., JANY U., PUDEL V., WEIß R., 1975, *Dunkelfeldforschung in Göttingen 1973/74*, Wiesbaden, Bundeskriminalamt [2].

SCHWIND H.-D., AHLBORN W., WEIß R., 1978, *Empirische Kriminalgeographie*, Wiesbaden, Bundeskriminalamt [3].

SCHWIND H.-D., AHLBORN W., WEIß R., 1989, *Dunkelfeldforschung in Bochum 1986/87*, Wiesbaden, Bundeskriminalamt [3].

SCHWIND H.-D., FETCHENHAUER D., AHLBORN W., WEIß R., 2001, *Kriminalitätsphänomene im Langzeitvergleich am Beispiel einer deutschen Großstadt*, Neuwied Kriftel, Luchterhand [3].

SCHWIND H.-D., ROITSCH K., AHLBORN W., GIELEN B. (Hrsg.), 1995, *Gewalt in der Schule*, Mainz, Weisser Ring [15].

SESSAR K., 2006, Warum man abends nicht das Haus verlässt. Kriminologische Ergebnisse aus einem europäischen Forschungsprojekt zu Unsicherheiten in Großstädten *in* OBERGFELL-FUCHS J., BRANDENSTEIN M. (Hrsg.), *Nationale und internationale Entwicklungen in der Kriminologie. Festschrift für Helmut Kury zum 65. Geburtstag*, Frankfurt/Main, Verlag für Polizeiwissenschaft, 265-293 [29].

STEPHAN E., 1976, *Die Stuttgarter Opferbefragung*, Wiesbaden, Bundeskriminalamt [1].

TESKE R. H. C., ARNOLD H., 1991, A comparative victimisation study in the United States and the Federal Republic of Germany: A description of the principal results *in* KAISER G., KURY H., ALBRECHT H.-J. (Eds.), *Victims and criminal justice*, 51, Freiburg, Eigenverlag Max-Planck-Institut für ausländisches und internationales Strafrecht, 3-44 [5].

WETZELS P. PFEIFFER C., 1996, Regionale Unterschiede der Kriminalitätsbelastung in Westdeutschland. *Monatsschrift für Kriminologie und Strafrechtsreform*, 79, 6, 386-405.

WETZELS P., ENZMANN D., MECKLENBURG E., PFEIFFER C., 2001, *Jugend und Gewalt*, Baden-Baden, Nomos [23].

WETZELS P., GREVE W., MECKLENBURG E., BILSKY W., PFEIFFER C., 1995, *Kriminalität im Leben alter Menschen*, Stuttgart, Verlag W. Kohlhammer [14].

WILMERS N., ENZMANN D., SCHAEFER D., HERBERS K., GREVE W. WETZELS P., 2002, *Jugendliche in Deutschland zur Jahrtausendwende: Gefährlich oder gefährdet? Ergebnisse wiederholter, repräsentativer Dunkelfelduntersuchungen zu Gewalt und Kriminalität im Leben junger Menschen 1998 – 2000,* Baden-Baden, Nomos [28].

Appendix

Comparison between police/social statistics and survey data

N°	Author	Year of Study	Territorial Scope and Focus	Comparison	Type of comparison
1	Stephan	1973	local, general	yes	police statistics: dark figure calculation
2	Schwind *et al.*	1973/1974	local; general	yes	police statistics: dark figure calculation
3	Schwind *et al.*	1975 – 1986 – 1998	local; general	yes	police statistics: dark figure calculation, structural comparisons
4	Kreuzer *et al.*	1990	no area specified; university students	no	
5	Arnold *et al.*	1981	regional / supranational; general	no	
6	Plate *et al.*	1982	local; general	yes	police statistics, social statistics: dark figure calculation; structural comparisons
7	Sessar, Boers	1984	local; general	yes	police statistics: model for fear of crime contrasting survey data

N°	Author	Year of Study	Territorial Scope and Focus	Comparison	Type of comparison
8	Kury	1989	national; general	yes, see n° 10; 18	police statistics, social statistics: structural comparisons
9	Aben	1990	local; general	yes	police statistics: structural comparisons
10	Kury *et al.*	1991	national; general	yes, see n° 8; 18	police statistics, social statistics: structural comparisons
11	Boers *et al.*	1991 – 1993 – 1995	national; general	yes	police statistics: structural comparisons
12	Kury *et al.*	1991/1992 – 1995/1996	local/regional; general	no	
13	Kräupl, Ludwig	1991/1992 – 1995/1996 – 2001/2002	local/regional general	yes	police statistics: dark figure calculation; structural comparisons
14	Wetzels *et al.*	1992	national; general	yes	police statistics: structural comparisons
15	Schwind *et al.*	1993	local; students	yes	no aggregated statistics but additional official survey data
16	Funk *et al.*	1994	local; students	yes	school statistics: multilevel analysis
17	Research Group Community Crime Prevention in Baden-Wuerttemberg	1994	local/regional; general	yes, partly (Freiburg)	police statistics: structural comparisons
18	Research Group Community Crime Prevention Baden-Wuerttemberg	1995	national; general	yes, see n° 8; 10	police statistics, social statistics: structural comparisons
19	Heinz *et al.*	1997	national; general	no	
20	Hermann *et al.*	1997 – 2004	local; general	yes	police statistics: structural comparisons
21	Kury *et al.*	1998	local; general	yes	police statistics: structural comparisons (discussion)
22	Kury *et al.*	1998	local; general	yes	police statistics: structural comparisons (discussion)
23	Wetzels *et al.*	1998	local; students	yes, see n° 34	police statistics: structural comparisons

N°	Author	Year of Study	Territorial Scope and Focus	Comparison	Type of comparison
24	Hermann, Dölling	1998	local; general	no	
25	Oberwittler *et al.*	1999	local; students	yes	police statistics, social statistics: multilevel analysis
26	Kury *et al.*	2000	local; general	yes	police statistics, social statistics: structural comparisons
27	Oberwittler *et al.*	2000	regional; students	yes	police statistics, social statistics: multilevel analysis
28	Wilmers *et al.*	2000	local/regional; general	no	
29	Sessar *et al.*	2001	local/supranational; general	yes	police statistics, social statistics: structural comparisons
30	Dreher *et al.*	2003	local; general	yes	police statistics: structural comparisons
31	Müller, Schröttle	2003	national; women	no	
32	Feltes, Goldberg	2003/2004	local; students	no	
33	Gallup/ Europe, Kury *et al.*	2005	national; general	yes	no separate comparisons for Germany; correlation police statistics and survey data
34	Pfeiffer *et al.*	2005	local/regional; students	yes, see n° 23	police statistics: structural comparisons

Comparing police data and victimisation surveys in Italy

Giovanni Sacchini

To describe the relationship between police statistics and victimisation surveys in Italy some dates can help us. The first victimisation survey – carried out since then under the name of *Indagini Multiscopo sulle famiglie 'Sicurezza dei citadini'* (a survey on the safety of citizens) – was presented just ten years before this workshop, on 1998 September 22nd. The data were disseminated by the *Istituto nazionale di statistica* (ISTAT, the National Institute of Statistic) during 1999 and have been made available to researchers starting in 2000 (Istat, 2000). The second edition of this investigation took place in 2002, whereas the third is currently under way (Istat, 2004; Muratore, Tagliacozzo, 2008) is presented a summary of the survey, both for the results and for the methodology).
What has been done actually in these ten years in comparative terms is fairly easy to summarise: there are no published works concerning, even indirectly, the comparison between data collected by the police and those collected with victimisation surveys. There are neither published works, nor an association or annual meeting where such topics could be publicly discussed among professionals. Consequently, we cannot rely upon it in our report, on any kind of researches or studies.
Because of the absence of material to be analysed, in this report we deal shortly with the reasons that may explain the difficulties of this situation, and without claiming to be complete, we shortly describe the two main aspects that make the work of analysis and comparison so difficult:

I. Organizational and institutional aspects

While the victimisation survey is completely managed by Istat (The National Institute of Statistics) in all its phases, the readings on crimes reported to police is part of the Minister of Interior, and Istat has only the task of spreading the data through its channels: the Yearbook paper (*Annuario di statistiche giudiziarie*) and the database available on its Web site (www.istat.it / justice; http://giustiziaincifre.istat.it).

Until 31.12.2003 crime registered by police forces was based on an information system organised on a Provincial level, summarising data of the three main police – The National police (PS), The *Carabinieri* and The Financial Police (GdF) – into a paper model, known bureaucratically as 'model 165' (Arcidiacono, Sacchini 2004, for a short description of the collection).

Since 2004 the system changed and a computerised system was finally adopted. Now the statistics are the product of a large information system that is called SDI (*Sistema Di Indagine*): this step has led to many innovations and some problems in giving continuity to the previous series and currently the data are presented for two different periods: 1984-2003 (model 165) and 2004-2007 (SDI). Technical information about the data produced with the SDI system are available from the Web site of the Statistical Office of the Minister of Interior (http://dait.interno.it/dcds/compendio04/nota%20delitti.htm).

One can says that there is more debate about the differences and similarities between 165 and SDI than there is between police and victimisation survey data, but this is a debate more underground than public and more among professionals than among academics: the place where this debate has been better shown is the 2007 Report of the Ministry of Interior (in particular on pp. 11-15) but there is an introductory discussion also in Sacchini (2008).

We can therefore say that the new internal data registration carried out by the Minister of Interior absorbs now much more attention than the comparison between victimisation data and the 165 model, partly for the different tasks that the Institutional players involved here – Istat and the Ministry of Interior – and partly for methodological difficulties that are peculiar to such comparisons (the latter will say little below).

II. Some methodological difficulties for comparisons

We are going to analyze some examples of these difficulties, grouped into five different paragraphs:

- The time when the event occurs;
- The definition of predatory crimes against individuals;
- The location where the crimes take place;
- The theft in the home (*burglary*);
- The attempted and completed offences.

1. The time when the event occurs

Time is the first, big, difference between the two sources: police data refer to a specific period – a year in the published data – while victimisation survey refers to a period before the day in which the person is interviewed. In the survey the reference periods are two: the 3 years before and the 12 months before the day of the interview.
This means that for the victimation survey the period of reference is strictly related to the period during which interviews are conducted. For example, in the second sweep, that of 2002, the period during which the 60.000 national interviews were conducted ranges from march 5th to October 22nd. On the other hand, the section of the questionnaire deeply investigating the characteristics of the event refers only to the month in which it has occurred, thus the interviews period make this information biased: in fact not all the 12 months of the year have the same probability of being investigated.
Starting from the original file, one can, of course, makes an estimation of the events during each momth of the year but it seems to be more an exercise than a comparison between the two sources.
Arcidiacono (2005) did this kind of exercise concerning to pickpocketings occurred in Emilia-Romagna and his work has taken some suggestions from a previous, introductory, article by Barbagli and Colombo (1999).

2. The definition of predatory crimes against individuals

The offences which could be compared are the following:

- *Borseggio* [pickpocketing];
- *Scippo* [bag snatching];
- *Furto di oggetti personali* [theft of personal objects, or theft without contact];
- *Rapina* [robbery].

Of course, the investigation of the crime in the survey is written in ordinary language while for the police the classification of events is a professional one and while it should create few problems for the first two offences referred above, on the contrary things are very complicated for the other ones.
For example, in the period 1984-2003, the thefts 'without contact' as defined in the survey, could be classificated by police on the basis of where they occur: 'in public offices' or 'rail' or end up in the wider category of 'other thefts', making in fact the comparison impossible.

Also the 'robbery' in the model 165 ends in the residual category of 'other robberies' even though some might be classified in the category of 'robbery to the detriment of couples or prostitutes': a category, the latter, already problematic in itself...
Starting with year 2004 (the first year of the SDI system), *Borseggio* [pickpocketing] and *Scippo* [bag snatching] have changed and improved their definition and things might improve a little for contactless theft and robberies. Actually, accepting a suggestion found in the Report of 2007 Ministry of the Interior, we can count the contactless theft as most of the 'other thefts': a residual category that is around a 40% of the total theft.
In the same way, it is possible to compare data concerning 'personal robberies' (victimisation) with those of the robberies that occurs 'on public roads' and for which the Report presents (for the first time) some interesting data. It must be said that SDI in the allocation of a theft in this or in that category works by a combination of certain information, present (or not), in some areas of the imputation masks and therefore we can say that the classification is a result mixing professional competence of information with some information constraints.
As one can see, the definition of crimes creates some problems, none of which is unbeatable, but which however is already a first obstacle, to which we must add the one related to the location where the crime took place.

3. The location where the crimes take place

The victimisation survey provides data referring to 100 residents (*prevalence and incidence rate*) in the place where they live (and where they are interviewed), whereas the data of the police for the years until 2003 refer to the place where the complaint (*denuncia*) was lodged; by 2004 (under SDI) they refer, in disseminating the data, to the place where the crime was actually committed, irrespective of where it was reported.
So, the different kinds of published statistics, as they are disseminated, are not directly comparable with each other.
In order to compare them, elaborations on the file (of victimisation) are necessary, because in that case it is possible to discover where people have been victimised: this path is accessible to researchers but could be referred only to the last incident (in the case of more than one incident per year).

4. The burglary

Also this offence, indicated by the victimisation' survey respondents, as 'the most fearful', in comparative terms presents some problems.

The main problem arises because victimisation survey suggests an important and useful distinction between the home involved in the crime, distinguishing between i) the main dwelling and ii) home for the holidays (or second home); a house, the latter, present in about 30% of Italian families.
In the collection of both the model 165 and the SDI, data presented do not take account into this distinction that detects important differences at a local level, in the sense that in recent years the rate per 100,000 residents of complaints for theft in dwelling was highest in those provinces where also the number of the second houses is the highest.
More than this, the victimisation survey data are presented with reference to the families residing in a certain place, regardless of where their second home is and therefore this makes even more difficult to compare the two figures.

5. Attempted and completed offences

Another difficulty which may arise in comparing the two kinds of data is that the victimisation survey distinguishes between those offences that were only attempted and that actually completed: in both cases, however, we have information relating to the fact of reporting or not, to the police.
The distinction between *attempted and completed offences* is also available in the SDI, but is not published and therefore a comparison with the data collected by SDI could be done trough a secondary analysis of the victimisation survey data. This solution would require considerable work on the file, but can be considered accessible to researchers through the method mentioned above for the location: in the case of repeat victimisation, however, it implies that the information is available only for the last incident, leaving all earlier occurrences unexplored.

*

The difficulties in comparing data from the two sources, both on the institutional-organisational side, and on the methodological one, in some cases seem to be surmountable, but the current situation of the two sources of information is such that much attention is devoted in the institutions involved and among researchers in improving the quality of data in the single source they are working with; hence the comparison with other sources of information at this stage is not considered interesting or important.
Moreover, the academic world had never shown much interest in this kind of comparison, given that this work does not seem to raise any interest in the public organisations that promote and use these two different sources.

The only experience of using comparison of these two different kinds of data of which we know are internal to some of the public organisations that use the data and seem to yield results satisfactory enough to read the variations of crimes based on time.
In this sense, the publication, scheduled for 2009, of the results produced with the third survey on 'safety of citizens' should allow a further stimulus for comparative work, even under the greater stability that the data collected by police forces with the SDI system are evidencing both nationally and locally.

References

ARCIDIACONO E., 2005, I borseggi, *Quaderni di Città sicure*, 11, 31, 111-143.

ARCIDIACONO E., SACCHINI G., 2004, Le fonti statistiche, *in* SELMINI R. (Ed.) *La sicurezza urbana*, Bologna, il Mulino, 65-78.

BARBAGLI M., COLOMBO A., 1999, Criminalità ufficiale, numero oscuro e delitti denunciati in Emilia-Romagna. Una stima, *Quaderni di Città sicure*, 5, 18, 211-225.

FISU – FORUM ITALIANO PER LA SICUREZZA URBANA, 2008, *Quindici anni di delittuosità e percezione della sicurezza nelle regioni italiane: 1991-2006*, Imola, Datacomp.

ISTAT, 2000, *Famiglie, abitazioni e sicurezza dei cittadini*, Roma, Istat.

ISTAT, 2004, *La sicurezza dei cittadini. Reati, vittime, percezione della sicurezza e sistemi di protezione*, Roma, Istat.

MINISTERO DELL'INTERNO – DIPARTIMENTO DELLA PUBBLICA SICUREZZA, 2007, *Rapporto sulla criminalità in Italia. Analisi, Prevenzione, Contrasto*, Roma, Ministero dell'Interno.

MURATORE M.G., TAGLIACOZZO G., 2008, *The Italian National Victimisation Survey*, *in* AROMAA K., HEISKANEN M., *Victimisation Survey in Comparative Prospective*, Heuni, Helsinki, 100-121.

SACCHINI G., 2008, *La delittuosità dal 1991 al 2006*, in FISU (2008), 35-81.

SELMINI R. (Ed.), 2004, *La sicurezza urbana*, Bologna, il Mulino.

Comparing crime data in the Netherlands

Karin Wittebrood

Crime is often viewed as a serious social problem. It leads to public outrage and concern, and tackling crime is high on the political agenda. However, it is not easy to obtain a clear picture of the nature, level and development of crime. The picture is heavily influenced by the media, who above all focus on the exceptional violent crimes. As a consequence, the seriousness and the level crime is easily overestimated. To gain an insight into the nature, level and development of crime in the Netherlands, a number of data sources are available. In this connection, the Netherlands occupies a special position; there are very few countries where annual information over a relatively long period is available, from a range of data sources.

The two most important data sources – both available over a longer period and often serving as a basis for policy in the field of police and justice – are the police statistics and the victimisation surveys[1]. The police registers crimes brought to their attention either via detection or following reporting. This information is then passed on to Statistics Netherlands (CBS) which organization has been registering the data since 1950, in the Police Statistics. Not all crimes committed are brought to the attention of the police. As a consequence, the police statistics are supplemented by victimisation surveys. In these surveys, a random sample of the population is asked whether they have been victims of certain (common) forms of crime, and thus provide an opportunity to determine the level and development of crime, over and above the police records. Since 1980, the CBS has been carrying out surveys of this kind.

In this paper we will start with a brief explanation of the generation of these two data sources. Next, on the basis of police statistics and the victimisation surveys – both provided by the CBS – we will present some figures on the level and development of crime in the Netherlands. We will show that both data sources give a different picture. In the remainder of the

1. Another important source of data which provides an insight into the level and development of crime is the so-called 'self report' study, in which a proportion of the population are asked whether they have committed certain crimes. Such studies are above all held amongst young people. In addition, they are rarely used for gaining an insight into the level of crime, but above all into the developments taking place within crime.

article, we summarize research which gives an explanation for the non-uniform development in crime between both data sources.

I. Police statistics and victimisation surveys in the Netherlands

1. Violence recorded by the police (police statistics)

The police records crimes which come to their attention through investigation, and which are reported to them by victims or witnesses. Not all crimes committed, however, are recognized as such by victims or witnesses, and the police is not always informed of all recognized crimes. In addition, not all crimes which come to the attention of the police either through investigation or reporting are in fact recorded. Factors which play a role in the recording of crime are the investigation policy of the police, and the prosecution policy of the Public Prosecutor's Office. Setting different priorities in criminal investigation or prosecution can have an influence on the level of recorded crime. Alterations in criminal law, publicity campaigns and the introduction of computer systems can also influence the level. All of these factors determine the proportion of the reported and investigated crimes which are recorded in a police report. Before a crime is recorded by the police, a number of filters have already been passed through. As a rule, the more serious forms of crime are relatively better recorded than the (commonly-occurring) less serious forms of crime.

Crimes recorded by the police are passed on to the CBS in the form of monthly completed report forms or (over the last few years) *via* automated records. Since 1950, these crimes have been contained in the police statistics, whereby crimes are broken down into crimes and groups of crimes as described in the various criminal codes. The number of police reports actually appearing in the police statistics for a specific crime will depend on the police administration. Doubt on the part of police officers about the correct legal qualification of the guidelines to be followed in completing the form for police statistics can play a role, in this connection. The police statistics therefore show crime as investigated or brought to the attention of the police and subsequently laid down in writing by the police and reported to the CBS. The violence recorded by the police, as contained in the police statistics, is therefore subject to a number of limitations which can above all play a major role in determining the level of violence. Firstly, it emerges – from victimisation surveys – that of violent crimes against persons, relatively few are reported to the police. From the victimisation survey of the CBS it emerged that in 2004, 34% of the victims reported the offence to the police (Wittebrood, 2006). The report rate differs enormously between offences: for threat for example the rate is 30% and for assault 40%, while for burglary it is 89%. Secondly, in particular in the case of violent crimes, there is considerable leeway for interpretation of the crime. Because of the ambivalent character of many of these crimes – more often than with other types of crime – it is not always clear precisely what has happened or whether a criminal act has indeed been committed. This has consequences for the willingness of the victims to report the event, as well as the registration policy of the police, and thus for official recording of the number of violent crimes.

2. Violence as experienced by the population (victimisation surveys)

In the Netherlands, victimisation surveys have for some considerable time represented an important source of information for gaining an insight into the level of crime as experienced by the population. In these surveys, people are asked whether they have been the victim of specific crimes. Crimes of which no report is made, or which are not recorded for some reason by the police can be reported in these surveys, by those questioned. The CBS has been carrying out national victimisation surveys in the Netherlands, since 1980. For the purpose of these surveys, a random sample is taken from private households, and questions are asked about victimisation of various forms of crime, to respondents aged 15 years and older. During the period 1980 to 1992, the Victim Survey (abbreviated in Dutch to ESM) was held, with a view to gaining an insight into the level of crime: first annually, and from 1984 onwards, every second year. By means of two questions, a determination is made as to whether the respondent has ever been a victim of a particular crime, and subsequently, in what year this took place. If the crime occurred in the reference period (*i.e.* the calendar year prior to the interview) a determination is also made of how often this situation arose. From 1992 onwards, the ESM was succeeded by the Justice and Security Survey (abbreviated in Dutch to ERV). In the ERV, the structure of the victim study was altered in a number of respects: the selection of respondents for example was altered, the survey was made continuous rather than relative to a specific period of the year, and the questions were changed. In posing these questions, a question is first asked about victimisation experience over the last five years. As in the ESM, for the reference period (*i.e.* the twelve months prior to the interview), a determination is made as to how often the respondent has been a victim of crime. Since 2005 the ERV is replaced by the safety Monitor. This new instrument differs on several methodological aspects from the previous. Consequently, a trend break arises between 2004 and 2005 (see Figure 1). Results from victimisation surveys relate primarily to individuals. On the basis of the information from the ESM and the ERV (the number of times people have been victims), an estimation is made by the CBS of the number of crimes committed amongst the Dutch population of 15 years and older, in a given year. As a consequence, the police figures and the victimisation surveys are more comparable. The use of victimisation surveys for estimating the level of crime is subject to limitations. Of essence is the fact that victimisation surveys are aimed at measuring victimisation against individuals and private households. Victim*less* crimes, such as possession of drugs and weapons, and speeding offences are automatically beyond the scope of the victimisation surveys. In addition, there are no details of crimes of which businesses and institutions are the victim (such as fraud and shoplifting) and crimes whereby the victim is no longer capable of participating in the survey (for example murder and manslaughter). Citizens below the age of fifteen years are also not included in the picture generated. Furthermore, in victimisation surveys, no legal crime descriptions are employed, because an attempt is made (in formulating the questions) to tie in with the perception of the respondents. This means that the descriptions employed generally allow a somewhat broader interpretation than the legal description of a crime. As is the case with the police figures, this limitation can above all become relevant in relation to violent crimes. A further limitation on the use of victimisation surveys, in describing the level of crime is that use is made of retrospective data[2].

II. The level and development of crime

Figure 1 shows the level and development of crime on the basis of the police statistics (1a, b, c, d). From 1950 until the end of the nineteen seventies, this number remained fairly stable. Then the level of crime grew considerably from 706,000 crimes in 1980 to 1.4 million in 2002. Since 2002 a drop in the crime rate can be seen. Figure 1 also shows how the level of crime has developed according to the data from victimisation surveys (1e, f, g, h). The first notable development is that the level of crime in the period 1980 to 2008 is considerably higher than on the basis of the police

2. for a detailed discussion, refer to Wittebrood, Nieuwbeerta, 2000.

statistics. In 1980, the police recorded for example 26,500 violent crimes, whilst according to the victimisation surveys, 654,000 violent crimes had taken place. In other words, more than 25 times as many crimes. The last couple of years the differences were smaller. In 2006, the police recorded 109,600 violent crimes, whilst according to the victimisation surveys 1,096,000 had been committed. The victimisation surveys show – as do the police statistics – that there was a rise in the level of crime, at the start of the 1980s. Subsequently, contrary to the police statistics, the overall level of violent crime fluctuates but remains stable.

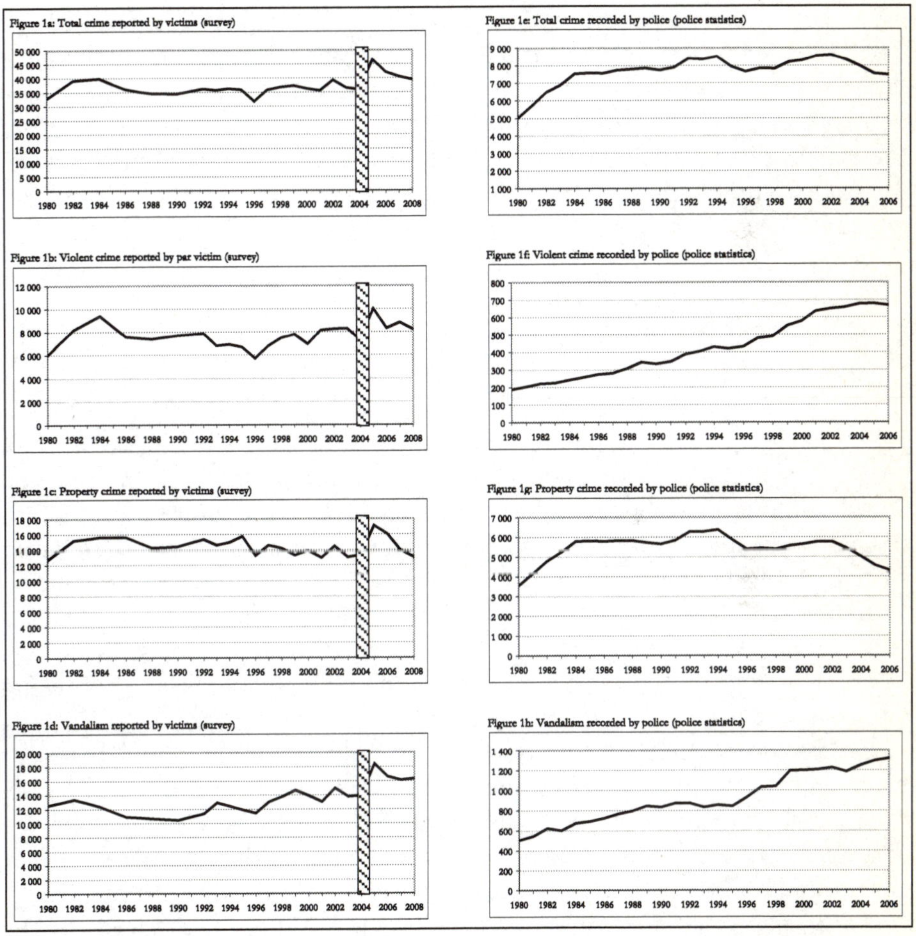

Figure 1: Trends in total crime, violent crime, property crime and vandalism according to police figures and victimisation surveys in the Netherlands 1980-2004 (levels per 100.000)

The picture which emerges from this description, concerning the level and development of crime in the Netherlands is therefore far from uniform. Firstly, the police statistics and victimisation surveys provide a different picture of the *level* of crime. Although the data from both sources cannot be easily compared, it is clear that the level on the basis of victimisation surveys is far higher, than on the basis of police figures. On the one hand, this is inherent in the functioning of the criminal justice system. Of all crimes notified by victims or witnesses, a report is not always made to the police, the police does not prepare a police report of all notified crimes, and not all completed police reports actually enter the official records. On the other hand, the information from both data sources differs because the definitions and measuring methods for the crimes diverge. In surveys, the descriptions of crime, for example, are far broader than the criminal law descriptions as employed by police and justice authorities. However, from the description, it emerges that not only the level of crime differs between the police statistics and the victimisation surveys, but also the *development* of crime.

III. Is crime increasing, or not?

In the literature of criminology, a number of different explanations are given for the fact that police statistics and victimisation surveys – in particular in terms of violent crime – show a different development in level. Some explanations assume that police statistics are more suitable for describing crime, whilst others suggest that victimisation surveys are better suited. In the Netherlands research on this topic has been carried out by Wittebrood and her colleagues (Wittebrood 1998; Wittebrood, Junger 2002; Wittebrood, Nieuwbeerta 2006). The main conclusions are described here. The generation of police statistics depends on the processes of filtering which take place in the criminal justice system. If there are more victims, if victims more often notify crimes to the police or if the police prepares more reports of the notification the police figures may show a rise in crime. To be able to say anything meaningful about the development of the willingness to report crimes, it is best to make use of the number of crimes committed and the number of crimes subsequently reported to the police. The CBS has calculated this information since 1980, on the basis of the victimisation surveys. In the victimisation surveys, the respondents who have been the victims of specific crimes were asked whether or not they reported the crime to the police. This information shows that the willingness to report crime has been slightly higher than in the nineteen eighties.

An increase in the number of reports the police prepares could be due to a general increase in productivity amongst the police, for example because police numbers are increasing, or as a result of automation. Equally, pressure on the police and justice authorities to achieve certain policy targets, for example by linking the allocation of funds to crime figures, could influence the willingness of the police to record crimes. But also changes in victim behaviour could be responsible for an increase in recorded crime. The development of number of recorded crimes can be derived from the victimisation surveys. This is because those respondents who indicate that they have reported a specific crime to the police are also asked whether they signed a police report or certificate of reporting. These informations show there is clear evidence of a rise in the willingness of the police to record crimes. The recording rate increases from 60% in the eighties to about 80% in 2004. This increase differs between types of crime: for violence it increases from 45% to 60% and for vandalism from 40% to 75%. For property crimes we only see an increase in the eighties; since then the recording rate is around 90%.
Wittebrood and Nieuwbeerta (2006) analysed the data of all 22 crime victimisation surveys, carried out by Statistics Netherlands in the period 1980-2004. Based on a scenario study they conclude that almost three-quarters of the increase in recorded crime are due to the fact that the police are recording more offences. The remaining quarter is due to the increase willingness of the public to report offences. Only 1% is attributable to an increase in the risk that citizens will become victims of crime.

*

On the basis of the above, it may be concluded that the rise shown by police figures in the level of crime, at least in part does not reflect a real increase. Indeed, it seems that the dark number – in other words the discrepancy between registered and non-registered crime – is becoming ever smaller. The most important reason for the fall in the dark number is that over the years, police records have improved considerably.
In order to gain a greater insight into the level and development of crime, it is important to continue studies in this field. For example, in the future, by determining in greater detail, in investigations, what forms of crime are and are not measured in the available data sources, an important contribution could be made to this improved understanding. Such investigations should not be focused only specifically on the Dutch situation, but should also be more general in nature. The finding that the police statistics and victimisation surveys represent a non-uniform development in crime is not typically Dutch. This means that explanations for this finding which relates specifically to the way in which Dutch data

sources are generated are not sufficient. In addition, account should be taken of the finding that the discrepancies in trends between police statistics and victimisation surveys apply particularly for violent crime.
In future investigations, a greater insight into the level and development of crime could be obtained by supplementing the data from police statistics and victimisation surveys with data from other sources. Over the last few years, information about violence, for example, has been collected more regularly and more systematically. Important sources are medical records of emergency department, Women's refuge centres and Doctors at advice centres. But also for other types of crime more information is available. The use of the greatest possible number of different data sources considerably increases the reliability of the findings about the level and development of crime.

References

WITTEBROOD K., 1998, *Cijfers omtrent geweld*, Den Haag, Raad voor Maatschappelijke Ontwikkeling.

WITTEBROOD K., 2006, *Slachtoffers van criminaliteit: feiten en achtergronden*, Den Haag, Sociaal en Cultureel Planbureau.

WITTEBROOD K., JUNGER M., 2002, Trends in violent crime: a comparison between police statistics and victimisation surveys, *Social Indicators Research*, 59, 2, 153-173.

WITTEBROOD K., NIEUWBEERTA P., 2000, Criminal victimisation during one's life course: the effects of previous victimisation and patterns of routine activities, *Journal of Research in Crime and Delinquency*, 37, 1, 91-122.

WITTEBROOD K., NIEUWBEERTA P., 2006, Een kwart eeuw stijging in geregistreerde criminaliteit: vooral meer registratie en nauwelijks meer criminaliteit, *Tijdschrift voor Criminologie*, 48, 3, 227-242.

Comparisons between survey estimates of crime and crimes recorded by the police: the UK position

Mike Hough, Paul Norris[1]

This paper summarises what can be said about comparisons between survey measures of crime and police statistics in the United Kingdom. The paper focuses almost entirely on surveys of victimisation, though there is a brief discussion about the relationship between surveys of self-reported offending and police statistics.

The paper falls into three parts. The first section describes the national crime surveys that cover the four countries of the United Kingdom:

- The British Crime Survey (BCS), covering England and Wales;
- The Scottish Crime Survey (SCS/SCVS), followed by the Scottish Crime and Justice Survey (SCJS), covering Scotland;
- The Northern Ireland Crime Survey (NICS), covering that part of Ireland which is part of the UK.

The second section describes the issues that have to be addressed in comparing survey estimates with police statistics and presents empirical findings on the relationships between recorded crime and survey estimates. This draws heavily on the BCS, though the same considerations apply to the other two surveys. A very short final section considers what can be said about comparing the results of surveys of self-reported offending to official crime statistics.

No extended discussion is required here of the rationale for surveys of victimisation. In brief, they permit a standardised approach to estimating crime trends that allows – in principle – consistency over place and time in estimating crime levels, including cases that are unreported to the police and unrecorded by the police. This is in contrast to police statistics of crime, where reporting and recording practices are known to vary over

1. The first part of this paper draws heavily on a paper prepared for, and funded by the Scottish Government, *Comparability of UK Crime Surveys: Paper 1: Comparison of Victimisation and Technical Details of Survey* by Paul Norris and Jackie Palmer (Scottish Centre for Crime and Justice Research). We are grateful to the Scottish Government for letting us reproduce parts of that paper here.

both place and time. Cross-jurisdictional variations in both reporting rates and police recording practice are of course very large.

I. The three national crime surveys

The three crime surveys which cover the UK are similar – sharing the same origins – but not identical. They vary in scale, in methodology, in coverage and in analysis. A brief review of the historical development of the different surveys serves to illustrate some of the reasons why comparability of estimates may be problematic.

1. The 1980s

The first BCS was conducted in 1982 and included data covering England, Wales and Scotland. Fieldwork in Scotland was conducted by the same company as that in England and Wales and used an identical questionnaire – though it covered only the (densely populated) southern part of Scotland. The absolute sample size was smaller in Scotland although the sampling fraction was much larger (5,000 for a population of 5 million as opposed to 10,000 for a population of 50 million). In the 1980s the BCS was conducted three times in England and Wales (in 1982, 1984 and 1988) and twice in Scotland (1982 and 1988). No crime survey data for Northern Ireland was collected in the 1980s, reflecting funding constraints and the priority that security issues attracted at that time.

2. The 1990s

The 1990s saw increasing divergence between the English and Scottish surveys. In England and Wales the BCS was conducted every other year from 1992 onwards. The BCS, now exclusively concentrating on England and Wales, had a steadily increasing sample size. The core sample size for the 2000 BCS was around 20,000. Booster samples aimed at providing accurate data about ethnic minorities and young people were also regularly included. The interview strategy of the BCS was changed in 1994 to one using Computer Assisted Personal Interviews (CAPI) and Computer Aided Self Interviewing (CASI) rather than paper questionnaires. The increased sample size of the BCS also allowed respondents to be split into smaller samples who were asked questions about different topics (victimisation questions are always asked of the full sample).

The first independent SCS was conducted in 1993 (a year later than the 1992 BCS due to delays associated with the development of the survey). Although similar to the 1992 BCS questionnaire, the 1993 SCS included several differences aimed at reflecting the differing context associated with the Scottish criminal justice system. The SCS sampling strategy and questionnaire design remained little altered for the 1996, 2000, and 2003 SCS.

The Northern Ireland Crime Survey began in the mid 1990s. A series of ad hoc crime surveys were conducted in 1994/95, 1998, 2001 and 2003/4. All these surveys had achieved sample sizes of just over 3,000 and were conducted using CAPI and CASI. The questionnaire used for NICS was closely modeled on that used for the BCS but the smaller sample size meant it was not possible to split the sample to cover as wide a range of topics as the BCS.

3. Recent developments

In 2001, the BCS moved to a continuous survey, sampling throughout the year, a move followed by NICS in 2005. The current BCS has a sample of around 47,000 a year while the NICS has a sample of 3,692 cases per year. As in the past, the NICS questionnaire is designed to closely mirror that of the BCS.

The 2004 SCS involved two separate surveys, a large sample telephone survey and a smaller face-to-face calibration survey. Following concerns about the reliability of the data collected in the telephone survey (Hope, 2005), the SCS reverted to personal interviews, now based on CAPI and CASI, a methodology that reflects those of the BCS and NICS. The last SCS was conducted in 2006. The Scottish Government has now redesigned the survey and re-launched it as the Scottish Crime and Justice Survey. The SCJS follows the BCS and NICS in moving to a continuous collection methodology and will also see an increase in sample size to a proposed level of 16,000. The questionnaire is similar to that of the BCS but by no means identical.

The differing development paths of the three surveys are also reflected in the ways in which they are managed and conducted. The BCS employs a relatively large in-house team who produce a wide range of reports based on the data collected. In contrast, the SCS and NICS have much smaller in-house teams whose work focuses on issues around levels of victimisation. In our view all three data-sets could have supported much more analysis, however, and the academic community in particular has missed opportunities for secondary analysis.

4. The samples

Table 1 provides an overview of the sampling design for the three UK crime surveys; focusing on size, target population and selection method. For the most part their sampling strategies are very similar and this suggests that comparison between the surveys should be possible. Key points to note are:

- The target population for all three samples is identical, covering those aged 16 and over who live in private households while excluding those who live in institutions
- The BCS includes booster samples for non-white respondents and those aged 16-24. This does not vitiate comparability but requires analytic choices to be made.
- The surveys use the best available sampling frame in their jurisdiction. The BCS uses the Small User Postcode Address File (PAF), as did the SCS. The SCJS is using the Multiple Occupancy Indicator whilst the NICS sample is drawn from the Land and Property Services list of private addresses.
- The BCS and the SCS use calibration weighting to try and ensure the make-up of their sample reflects that of the wider population; and in all three surveys other weights are also applied, for example to ensure that the sample represents individuals rather than households, when necessary.

5. Response rates

Another potential source of bias is in terms of who chooses to answer the survey, which may influence the accuracy and comparability of estimates of victimisation. To some extent the use of weighting can help to adjust for non-response. The BCS has always had a good response rate, and this remains at 75% – or just over[2]. The SCS achieved a response rate of 70.5% in 2006, and figures for the 2008 SCJS will emerge in 2009. The 2006/07 sweep of NICS achieved 64%.

2. The contractors are required to hit a target of 75%, and thus invest considerable effort to ensure that they do so.

Aspect of Sampling	British Crime Survey 2005/ 2006	Northern Ireland Crime Survey 2005	Scottish Crime Survey 2006
Target Sample Size	46,000 (minimum 1,000 in each police force area)	4,000	5,000
Eligible Percentage	91.7	89.4%	90.1%
Response Rate	75.2%	67.5%	70.5%
Actual Sample	47,479	3,692	4,948
Sampling Frame (Households)	Small User Postcode Address File. Excludes those in institutions such as halls of residence, care homes, prisons or the armed forces.	Land and Property Services list of private addresses. Excludes those in institutions except those who live in private households on such sites.	Small User Postcode Address File. Excludes those in institutions such as halls of residence, care homes, prisons or the armed forces.
Sampling Frame (Individuals)	Random adult aged 16 and over in chosen household (no replacements allowed). See also youth booster sample below.	Random adult aged 16 and over in chosen household (no replacements allowed).	Random adult aged 16 and over in chosen household (no replacements allowed).
Stratification	Postcodes sectors assigned to Police Force Area giving two levels of clustering. Population density and proportion of those aged 16-74 in non manual occupations	n/a	Postcodes sectors assigned to Police Force Area giving two levels of clustering. Population density and proportion of those aged 16-74 in non manual occupations
Clustering	PSU was postcode sectors (sectors with less than 500 addresses joined with neighbours). 32 addresses per PSU. 50% PSU from previous survey maintained but with different addresses. Only 16 addresses issued for PSUs where non-white population above 26% in 2001 census. – compensated for by duplication of PSUs	n/a	PSU was postcode sectors (sectors with less than 500 addresses joined with neighbours). 22 addresses per PSU.
Timing of Survey	Continuous – April 2005 to June 2006. Allows estimates each quarter.	Continuous – January 2005 to December 2005	June to December 2006 with a reference period since April 2005
Booster Sample	Booster sample for non-white respondents – selected through focused enumeration (target 3000 interviews). Booster sample for those aged 16-24. Selected from core households where the "main respondent" was not aged 16-24 and other people of this age are present in the property (target 2000 interviews).	None	None

Table 1: Sampling Design in UK Crime Surveys

6. Questionnaires

All three surveys follow the convention of asking a series of screener questions to establish if respondents have experienced particular forms of victimisation in the 12-month period[3] before interview; respondents who indicate they have experienced victimisation are asked to provide further information to allow the incident(s) to be fully coded in the same way as the police would have recorded the incident, and to provide more information about the nature of victimisation. This is done *via* 'victim forms'.

The three surveys use screener questions which are broadly comparable in scope, ordering and wording. There are small differences. For example there is no screener question referring to sexual attacks in the NICS and the Scottish surveys do not differentiate between whether or not household crimes occurred at their present or previous address. There are differences in the nature and number of questions preceding the screens, which could affect the 'productivity' of the questions[4].

The BCS Technical Report for 2006/07 describes the "life calendar" listing key events during the reference period to try and aid in accurate recall (Bolling *et al.*, 2008). Although no mention of a similar instrument is made in the NICS Technical Report, communication with the NICS team shows that their fieldworks do make use of a similar resource. No calendar instrument appeared to have been used in the SCS.

The 2006/07 BCS Technical Report notes, *the victim form is the key to the estimate of victimisation*... (26). Besides providing detailed information for possible analysis, the aim of the victim form is to provide sufficient detail about an incident to allow it to be accurately coded. The Victim Forms associated with all three surveys collect information about three broad issues (indeed the description in the SCS and BCS technical reports is almost word for word identical). Firstly, an exact month for the incident is collected to ensure that it has occurred within the time frame being used for calculating victimisation rates. Secondly, an open ended description of the incident is collected (this allows the respondent to describe exactly what happened and is important for the subsequent coding procedure). Finally, a series of closed questions are used to collect key characteristics of the offence. The answers to these questions may contribute to the coding

3. Until the surveys moved to continuous interviewing throughout the year, they were mounted in the first part of the calendar year and used the previous calendar year as the reference period.
4. For example, asking people about crime worries in advance of the screener might sensitize them to specific forms of victimisation.

process but also allow for additional analysis to be undertaken looking at issues such as the context in which an offence occurred.

While the victim forms associated with all three surveys cover the same broad issues their exact content does vary. The BCS consists of two designs of victim form, a long form and a short form. The long form design is used for the first three victim forms a respondent is asked to complete and the shorter form for incidents 4 to 6. The long design includes additional questions aimed at gaining a more complete understanding of an incident, the differences between the long and short forms do not influence the process of coding offences. It is rather that the long-form collects additional information which can be used for other analysis. The NICS also employs both long and short victim forms, although both of these are more strictly comparable to the short form used in the BCS. The NICS have excluded questions which are included on the BCS long form where they believed they would not generate usable data given the smaller sample size of the NICS. In addition, removing these questions allowed for the inclusion of additional topics within NICS, in particular around issues of performance measurement (personal communication with Brian French). The 2006 SCS used only one design of victim form (in contrast to some previous sweeps where mixtures of long and short forms appear to have been used). The SCS Technical Report draws attention to how this form as remained broadly unaltered over time. The exact contents of the SCS victim form has diverged from that of the BCS since 1993. However, these changes do not affect the basic information collected about victimisation.

7. Victim forms

The maximum number of victim forms respondents are asked to answer varies between surveys. Six forms are completed in the BCS and NICS while only 5 are completed in the SCS. Given that the information recorded on the victim forms is used as the basis for coding offences and calculating victimisation statistics, allowing respondents in different surveys to answer varying numbers of victim forms may reduce the comparability of estimates between regions. However, it is important that this is not overstated as in reality very few respondents complete the maximum allowable number of victim forms. For instance, only 0.9% of those in the SCS sample completed 5 victim forms (2.9% of victims) while only 0.2% of the BCS sample (1% of victims) completed 5 or 6 victim forms. It is highly likely that some, although not many, respondents in each survey will have experienced more types of victimisation than can be covered in the maximum number of victim forms they are allowed to complete. In this case, victim forms are asked about offences based on a priority ranking. If different surveys placed offences in different orders of importance this could influence which types of victimisation respondents are asked about and reduce comparability between surveys. None of the technical reports explicitly state the order in which offences are prioritised when victim forms are being answered. However, for all three surveys the order is broadly the inverse of that in which screener questions are asked.

8. Calculating victimisation rates and 'series' incidents

Measures of victimisation are commonly expressed two forms: prevalence rates (the percentage of individuals who have being victimised at least once) and incidence rates (a count of the number of victimisations per 10,000 people). The calculation of incidence rates is likely to be affected by how repeat victimisation is recorded. All three surveys have traditionally asked respondents who have suffered a given type of victimisation more than once if they believe the incidents were related and as such can be treated as a 'series'. This approach is historical and was done largely to reflect the way in which the criminal justice systems treated repeat victimisation of a person (or property) by a single perpetrator as a single ongoing incident. The extent to which these figures are now comparable to official figures should be considered to see if this approach to counting is still relevant following the introduction of new police recording procedures. In the calculation of incidence rates, repeat victimisation is capped to ensure that no extreme values unduly influence the overall estimate. It has being argued that this causes crime surveys to under-estimate the real level of victimisation[5]. In terms of ensuring comparability between the different UK crime surveys, the important issue is that capping should occur in the same way. This is the case, as all surveys cap counts at 5 incidents per series. However, it is important to note that comparisons based on capped incidence rates may not reflect the true victimisation rates in each region if repeat victimisation (above the capping level) is more prevalent in one of the jurisdictions.

9. Coding of Offences

The objective of offence coding is to assign those crimes which individuals report during a crime survey to a category comparable to those used in

5. For a discussion of this see Pease, Farrell 2007.

police recorded crime data and to enable the calculating of victimisation rates. This classification is based on the information respondents were asked to provide during the "victim form" part of the survey. Each survey has a set of coding instructions which explain how to use the information on the victim forms to arrive at a final offence classification. Since only one crime is recorded for each victim form, the most important issue in the calculation of victimisation estimates is which offence is most important when an incident involves a respondent being the victim of more than one 'crime'. For instance, should a burglary which has involved violence be recorded as a burglary or an assault? If the coding instructions used by different surveys vary in their interpretation of such incidents then it could be expected to influence the final estimates of victimisation levels.

The coding procedures used across the surveys are generally similar. They are derived from the coding schedule devised (by the author) for the first BCS, and those for the BCS have changed little since. They involve specially trained coders whose work is regularly checked for quality control purposes and difficult to code cases are referred to the respective government agency (*i.e* Home Office, Scottish Executive etc). The BCS experimented with an initial coding stage where a computer system attaches a provisional coding to each incident, but this was not adopted. Although the final coding decisions are made by the individual coders – using all the information on a victim form and with reference to the coding manual – there could be a possibility that the pre-coding of forms by the software could influence the decisions reached by individual coders.

The NICS coding instructions are a near identical match to those for the BCS with a couple of minor differences. The coding manual for the SCS does diverge to a greater extent from those for the BCS and NCIS. These differences reflect real differences in the nature of legal proceedings in Scotland. These differences have become more pronounced since 2003 as prior to this coding was largely based on English Law.

10. How comparable are the surveys' estimates of crime

The three surveys clearly have many similarities. They have similar samples, similar strategies for screening their samples, and similar questionnaire wording. It is probably fair to say that comparisons in trends over time can safely be made for most of the types of crime measured by the three surveys. It is more questionable whether there is *strict* comparability between the surveys in prevalence rates and – in particular – in incidence rates for a given year for a given type of crime, given divergences over time in design and analysis decisions. In other words the point estimates of incidence and prevalence may be less comparable than the direction of trend.

II. Comparing survey estimates of crime with recorded crime statistics

So far this paper has considered how the three UK national crime surveys generate estimates of prevalence and incident rates for different types of crime. Comparing survey estimates with statistics of crimes recorded by the police involves two further stages of analysis:

- Grossing up incidence rates to cover the population from which the sample is drawn;
- Adjusting the police counts of crime to improve comparison with the survey estimates.

1. Grossing up

This is conceptually straightforward, but technically challenging. Two accurate multipliers are needed: the total number of households and the total number of adults (*i.e.* those aged 16 plus) in the jurisdiction[6]. In reality, government estimates are neither precise nor accurate. They are generally drawn from decennial census data, with adjustments conducted throughout the inter-census period. The census itself does not yield a complete count of people and households. Any inaccuracies in the multipliers clearly jeopardize the integrity of point estimates, and variations over time in the degree of inaccuracy may compromise trends.

To take an example, the BCS incidence rate for domestic burglary (including attempts) in 2007/2008 was 309 per 10,000 households. Applying this rate to the household multiplier yields a total of 729,466 – which is rounded to 729,000 to avoid spurious precision. The same process can be carried out to estimate the number of burglaries *reported to* the police.

6. The 2007/2008 BCS for example, had a multiplier of 23,607,317 for the number of households, and 43,839,000 for the number of individuals aged 16 or over.

2. Adjusting the police counts of crime

The first stage in adjusting the police count of crimes to be compared with survey estimates is to identify the 'comparable sub-set' of crimes covered by both datasets. Crime surveys cover experience of crimes committed against individuals and their personal property. The police statistics obviously cover a large number of crime categories that are not counted – or not counted with sufficient accuracy to enable comparisons – by crime surveys. Important categories are:

- Shoplifting and other commercial theft;
- Burglary (non-dwelling);
- Criminal damage committed against institutional or commercial property;
- Fraud and forgery[7];
- Drug offences;
- Murder.

The remaining offence categories are referred to in BCS publications as 'the comparable sub-set' or the recorded crime BCS comparator. They comprise: vandalism (criminal damage), burglary (dwelling), attempted burglary (dwelling), theft from motor vehicles, theft of motor vehicles, attempted theft of and from motor vehicles, bicycle theft, wounding, common assault, robbery and theft from the person. Some but not all of these crime categories need further adjustment to exclude crimes that could not have been identified by crime surveys. Personal and household crimes are treated differently[8], for personal crimes, downward adjustments are needed to reflect the fact that the police counts of crime include, and the surveys exclude:

- Offences committed against those under the age of 16;
- Offences committed against those living in institutions (eg student halls of residence, hospitals, prisons and military establishments).

Amongst household crimes, vehicle theft and vandalism are adjusted downward to remove thefts involving commercial vehicles and vandalism committed against organizations or institutions. Full details of the adjustments are provided in Appendix 1.

Once all these adjustments are made, comparisons can be made between crime survey estimates and police statistics to identify, within the

7. Victims are often institutional, and even where they are not, it is hard to drawn clean boundaries between incompetence and criminal intent where people deliver sub-standard goods or services.
8. 'Personal crimes' are those where respondents report only about their own experience. There is no 'proxy reporting' of other household members' experience of assault, for example. 'Household crimes' are those where the entire household is treated as victim, such as burglary, vehicle theft and (even) bicycle theft.

comparable subset: the proportion of crime that goes unreported; the proportion of crime that goes reported but unrecorded and the proportion of crime that is recorded. Figure 1 shows rates of reporting to the police for the comparable subset. Equivalent incidence rates for these offences can be computed and then grossed up to reflect the population as a whole. Combining these estimates with the adjusted police figures yields three sets of estimates: all crimes in the comparable subset; crimes that are reported; and crimes that are *recorded.*

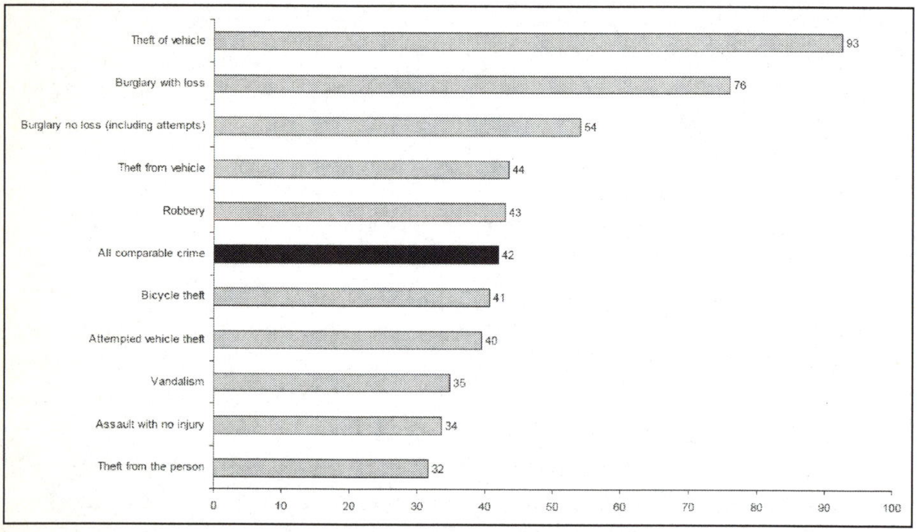

Source: Kershaw, Nicholas and Walker, 2008

Figure 1: Reporting to the police, England and Wales, 2007/2008

Figure 2 shows estimates for 2007/08 and for previous years in England and Wales, with values for reported, recorded and 'all BCS' indexed to 1981 values as 100%. It illustrates how reporting and recording rates have varied over time. In very general terms, reporting rates increased throughout the 1980s and then stabilised. Police recording have fluctuated in different ways at different times. In the early 1990s there is evidence that the police – possibly under political pressure to show falls in crime – reduced their recording rates. From 1998 onwards, a series of policy changes encouraged the police to adopt policies of full recording, which explains the rather erratic recent trends in recorded crime in the five years after 1998, These changes now appear to have bedded in, and recently (since 2004) all three trend lines in Figure 2 show a broadly consistent pattern.

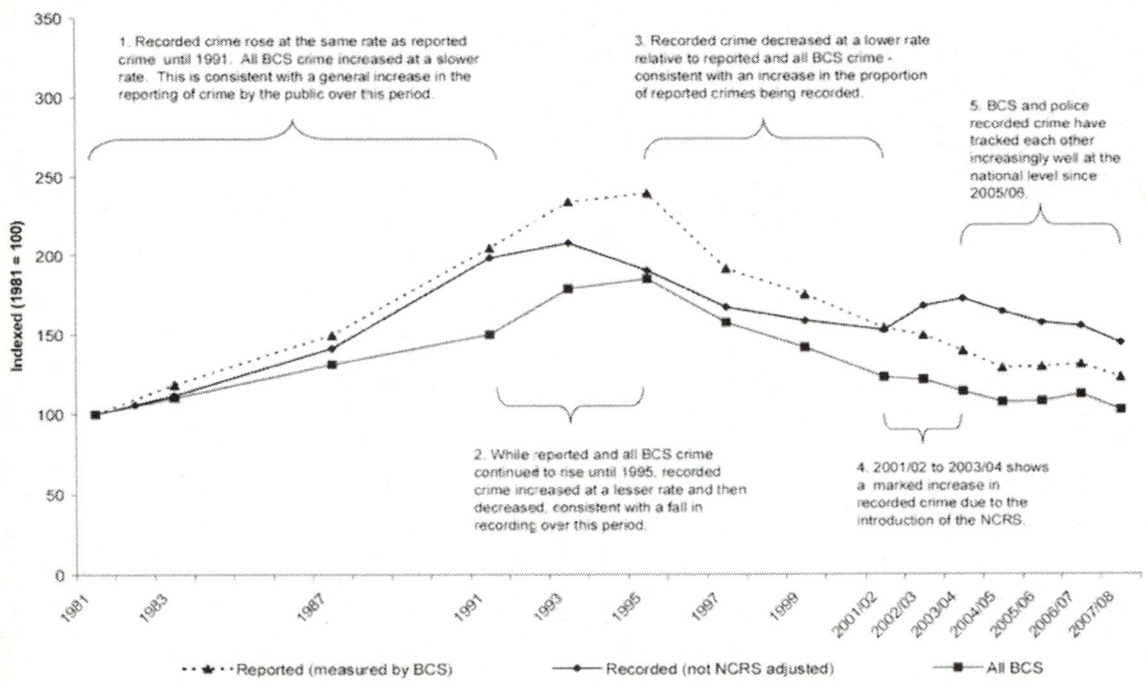

1. BCS estimates of incidents for 1991 to 2007/08 are based on estimates of population and the number of households in England and Wales that have been revised in light of the 2001 Census. For more information please see the Glossary.
2. From 2001/02, reported and all BCS crime relate to interviews carried out in that financial year and incidents experienced in the 12 months prior to interview. Recorded crimes relate to incidents in the 12 months up to the end of September of that financial year. This is so that the recorded crime data are centred on the same period as reported and all BCS crime.
3. To compare BCS and police recorded crime figures it is necessary to limit both to a set of offences that are covered by both series (comparable subset).

Source: Kershaw, Nicholas and Walker, 2008

Figure 2: Comparing BCS trends with police statistics

3. How robust are the resultant comparisons?

It is hard to say how reliable crime surveys are in estimating the extent of unreported and unrecorded crime, because there is no independent benchmark against which to assess them. However the plausibility and consistency of estimates over time is impressive, given the number of stages – and the number of assumptions that are made – in the estimation process. Consider these two examples, taken from the 2004/05 BCS for England and Wales[9]:

	Vehicle theft	*Burglary with loss (dwelling)*
Incidence rate	93/10 000 households	143/10 000 households
Grossed up	214 000 BCS crimes	327,000 BCS crimes
Reporting Rate	95%	77%
Reported	202 000 BCS crimes	251,000 BCS crimes
Unadjusted police comparator	202 000 crimes	262,000 crimes
Adjusted comparator	186 000 crimes	262, 000 crimes
Recording rate	92%	104%

How much effort needs to be expended on getting a reliable and precise estimate of the *volume* of unreported and unrecorded crime is a question of judgment. The BCS has provided a powerful tool for understanding trends in reporting and recording, and yet, ironically, the existence of the BCS – combined with successive changes in policy about the crime recording process – has resulted in a confusing array of indices of crime. As a result, public trust in crime statistics is at an all time low.

What is clear, however, is that most of the turbulence in the recording process has affected the less serious categories of crime. Figure 3 shows that indexed trends for serious recorded crime largely track the trend for all BCS crime – with the exception of the period in the early 1990s, when recording rates fell even for serious offences. The upward trend in *all* recorded crimes around the turn of the century is largely an artifact of changes in the recording process.

9. Estimates are rounded.

1 The police recorded serious crime subset comprises most serious violence against the person, most serious sexual offences, robbery, burglary, and theft or unauthorised taking of a motor vehicle.

Source: Kershaw, Nicholas and Walker, 2008

Figure 3: Trends in 'All BCS', all recorded crime and a 'serious subset' of recorded crime

The Scottish and Northern Irish surveys have restricted themselves largely to comparison of trends survey and police, without any sustained attempt to achieve precise comparability in volume estimates. In other words, they have avoided the rather tortuous processes of grossing up to the population and fine-tuning recorded crime figures to improve comparability with their surveys.

One problem that none of the three surveys has addressed satisfactorily is the periods of comparison for surveys and police statistics. There is a 'rolling reference period' for interviews conducted in any one financial or calendar year. In other words, respondents who are interviewed on 1 April 2007 are asked to report incidents happening between 1 April 2006 and 30 March 2007. Those who are interviewed on 30 March 2008 are asked to report incidents happening between 30 March 2007 and 29 March 2008. In other words the interviews in that financial year collectively cover a reference period of 24 months. The resultant estimates are compared with the 12 months' of police statistics for the financial year in which the interviews were conducted.

There are two problems, neither of them readily soluble. The first is that strictly speaking, like is not being compared with like. A rolling average covering a two year period is being compared with an annual total. The second is that the rolling average that is actually used is not the best available one: the BCS reports suggest that it would be better to compare police statistics in any given financial year with survey estimates for the 12 month period starting six months later than the financial year. To date, the Scottish Surveys and the NICS have sensibly sidestepped these complicated – and presentationally challenging – issues associated with rolling reference periods.

III. Surveys of self-reported offending

Finally we should say a little about surveys of self reported offending. The United Kingdom, and England and Wales in particular, has considerable experience of these surveys. For example, there is the Youth Lifestyles Survey, which provides information on both victimisation and offending for a sample of teenagers and young adults. Two sweeps have been conducted, and a third may be conducted when resources are available. There is also the Offending and Criminal Justice Survey, a survey of young people's experience as victims and offenders (Budd *et al.*, 2005a & b; Hayward, Sharp, 2004; Sharp *et al.*, 2006; Wood, 2005). There has also been a – methodologically more problematic – Arrestees Survey, which includes drug testing and self-report interviewing of offenders in police stations. There is also the Citizenship Survey, which has some relevance to the criminal justice system.

None of these surveys is likely to yield any fine-turned estimates of crimes committed, that can sensibly be compared with crimes recorded by the police. The problem is partly that serious and persistent offending is concentrated in a small sub-population, and even very large population surveys will reach only a small proportion of these people, assuming 100% response rates. Even with 100% response rates, sampling error would be very large. However the problem is compounded by the fact that offending groups are amongst the hardest for surveyors to reach. It is further compounded by problems of recall, and problems of honesty, that will affect people who are being asked to report on illegal behaviour spanning a period of 12 months.

This is not to suggest that self-report surveys are valueless. They have been very useful in yielding estimates of forms of minor crime that people are ready to admit to. They also provide the best available national indicators of the prevalence of the use of the less dangerous illicit drugs, notably cannabis. But it is quite clear that they will never be able to yield robust estimates of the volume of serious crime that are precise enough to compare with statistics recorded by the police.

References

ALLEN J., RUPAREL C., 2006, *Comparing BCS estimates and police counts of crime*, London: Home Office, [http://www.homeoffice.gov.uk/rds/pdfs06/comparingbcs.pdf].

BOLLING K., GRANT C, BOLLING K., SINCLAIR P., 2008, *2006/07 British Crime Survey (England and Wales) Technical Report Volume I*, [http://www.homeoffice.gov.uk/rds/pdfs07/bcs0607tech1.pdf].

BUDD T., SHARP C., MAYHEW P., 2005a, *Offending in England and Wales: First results from the 2003 Crime and Justice Survey,* Home Office Research Study No. 275, [http://www.homeoffice.gov.uk/rds/pdfs05/hors275.pdf].

BUDD T., SHARP C., WEIR G., WILSON D., OWEN N., 2005b, *Young people and crime: findings from the 2004 Offending, Crime and Justice Survey,* Home Office Statistical Bulletin 20/05, [http://www.homeoffice.gov.uk/rds/pdfs05/hosb2005.pdf].

FARRELL G., PEASE K, 2007, The sting in the tail of the British Crime Survey: multiple victimisation, *in* HOUGH M., MAXFIELD M.(eds), *Surveying Crime in the 21st Century,* Cullompton, Willan Publishing, 33-53.

HAYWARD R., SHARP C., 2004, *Young people and anti-social behaviour: Findings from the 2003 Crime and Justice Survey*, Home Office Findings 245, [http://www.homeoffice.gov.uk/rds/pdfs05/r245.pdf].

HOPE S., 2005, *Scottish Crime and Victimisation Survey: calibration exercise – a comparison of survey methodologies*, Research report for the Scottish Executive, Edinburgh, Scottish Executive, [http://www.scotland.gov.uk/Resource/Doc/47121/0020932.pdf].

KERSHAW C., NICHOLAS S., WALKER A., 2008, *Crime in England and Wales 2007/08,* Home Office Statistical Bulletin 07/08, London: Home Office, [http://www.homeoffice.gov.uk/rds/pdfs08/hosb0708.pdf].

SHARP C, ALDRIDGE J., MEDINA J., 2006) *Delinquent youth groups and offending behaviour: findings from the 2004 Offending, Crime and Justice Survey*, Home Office Online Report 14/06, [http://www.homeoffice.gov.uk/rds/pdfs06/rdsolr1406.pdf].

WOOD M., 2005, *The victimisation of young people: findings from the Crime and Justice Survey, 2003*, Home Office Findings 246, [http://www.homeoffice.gov.uk/rds/pdfs05/r246.pdf].

Appendix 1 – Comparing BCS estimates and police counts of crime 2005/2006[10]

1. Background

The police and the British Crime Survey (BCS) measure crime in significantly different ways. The offences that are recorded by the police are a subset of the crimes that are reported to them, and those reported are a subset of the crimes that actually occur. The first BCS in 1982 was carried out partly to uncover the 'dark figure' of crime that was not being picked up in the existing police statistics.

The BCS is a general population survey that asks about respondents' experiences of victimisation in order to make an estimate of the extent of crime. However, as a household survey, there are some crimes that it cannot cover or cannot cover effectively (murder is an obvious category, fraud and crimes against businesses are others). There is, however, a significant group of crimes that both the BCS and police recorded crime consider in a comparable way (these represented 78% of all the crimes covered in the BCS in 2005/06). This document sets out what those crimes are and describes the adjustments that have been made to the two data sets in 2005/06 to make the categories as closely comparable as possible.

2. The comparable subset of crimes

From the first sweep of the BCS in 1982, there have been a group of crimes that have been recorded by the police and coded by the BCS in a way similar enough to be able to make comparisons. The broad categories are:

- Vandalism (criminal damage)
- Burglary (attempts and with entry)
- Vehicle-related theft (theft of, theft from and attempted theft of or from a motor vehicle)
- Bicycle theft
- Theft from the person
- Wounding
- Robbery

10. This appendix is extracted from Allen and Ruparel (2006).

In addition, as a result of changes to recorded crime counting rules in 1998, two further categories have been included since that point, thereby creating a new comparable subset:

- Common assault
- Vehicle interference (which has been added to attempts of/from vehicles)

The population for the BCS is those aged 16 and over in private households in England and Wales, and as such it does not cover personal crime where the victim is under 16 years, nor does it cover crimes against commercial targets, unlike police recorded figures. In order to take account of these and other differences and make the crime subset more comparable, adjustments are made to the recorded crime data to bring it into line with BCS data.

3. Adjustment methodology

Questionnaire to police forces

Some of the required adjustments to the recorded crime data were made using estimates based on data held by the individual police forces that is not provided to the Home Office as standard. In order to collate this data, a questionnaire is sent annually to the 43 Home Office police forces and the British Transport Police. Data requested in that questionnaire includes the number of violent offences in the comparable categories that are against those under 16 years, the proportion of criminal damage that is against private households and the proportion of vehicle-related theft that is against commercial targets. Responses were received from all 43 forces and the British Transport Police for the 2005/06 adjustments. However, because the data requested for the adjustments is not included in the main returns to the Home Office, not all forces collect the data, and, among those that do, there may be inconsistencies in the method of collection.

Presented in Table 1 are the overall response rates for the individual adjustment estimates. Some of these, particularly in relation to assessments of the number of offences against commercial targets, are relatively low. Where there is also doubt around the quality and consistency of the data received, the final adjustments do not use the questionnaire as a source of data (see next section for a description of the final adjustments).

Number against commercial targets	
Theft from vehicles	66
Theft of vehicles	66
Vehicle interference	64
Number against private households	
Criminal damage	55
Number against under 16s	
Wounding	98
Common assault (no injury)	100
Robbery	100
Theft from the person	100

Table 2: Response rates (%) for adjustments within offence categories (44 forces total)

Where the data from the questionnaire to forces is used, estimates of the proportion of total offences in a particular category that were against private or commercial targets or under 16s were calculated by taking a weighted average across the forces for which data was available. For each offence category, this involved taking the proportion that were against commercial or private targets or under 16s for a particular force and weighting that proportion by the total number of offences that that force recorded in 2005/06 relative to the total for all forces across all offences. The average of these weighted proportions better reflects the wide variation between forces in numbers of offences recorded.
Where it has been decided that the questionnaire data is not reliable, assumptions have been based on the best available data, or, where recent data was not available, considerations of maintaining continuity in the methodology from previous years.

Other data sources

In addition to those made for under 16s and private households or commercial targets, adjustments are also made to recorded burglary and vehicle-related theft offences to separate out attempts in these categories and thereby bring them in line with the BCS. The adjustments in the past have defined attempts as those offences where the loss or damage was of 'nil value', as this category is made up largely of attempts and is recorded centrally by the Home Office. 'Nil value' offences are no longer collected centrally however, so the adjustments for 2004/05 apply the same proportion as the most recent available data. The proportion of offences that the police define specifically as 'attempts' is now collected centrally instead, this data has been used in part in the adjustments for 2005/06.

Reference periods

The move to continuous sampling on the BCS in 2001 has meant that the reference periods between recorded crime and BCS estimates are not identical. The latest BCS interviews in 005/06 provide a range of 12-month recall periods over two years that centre on March 2005. The most comparable period for recorded crime is for the year to September 2005 (as this also provides data centred on March 2005).
The adjustments are made to recorded crime for the year to September 2005, but the calculation of those adjustments is based on data from the questionnaire to police forces that refers to financial years. To take account of this, adjustment figures are calculated for the financial years 2004/05 and 2005/06 and an average is taken of these to be applied to the year to September 2005 recorded crime numbers.

Interpretation

Overall, the comparisons of recorded crime and BCS estimates provide a useful assessment of the gap between crimes committed and their recording by the police. However, the lack of reliable data in some areas and the differences in reference period between the data sources means some care needs to be taken with interpretation of results.

4. Final adjustments made in calculations

This section presents the full list of adjustments made in the comparison of recorded crime and BCS estimates, and the codes from each source that comprise the categories.

- British Transport Police (BTP) offences that are not cleared up are added to the totals listed here for these adjustments. BTP figures here are an average across the financial years 2004/05 and 2005/06, for these adjustments only, hence will not match totals of recorded crime figures in Crime in England and Wales 2005/06.
- Data for recorded crime is for the year to September 2005, and from 2005/06 interviews for the BCS.
- Adjustments to the recorded crime figures can be made to make the categories comparable to the period before the introduction of the counting rule changes of 1998. These adjustments are applied when looking at the old comparable subset in order to look at trends back to 1982. The same ratio (of number of crimes in each offence category

under the new rules to the number under the old rules) that was found in the 1999 calculations has been applied in the calculations in subsequent years.

Vandalism (Criminal Damage)

i. Including BTP figures, the unadjusted total recorded crime figure was 1,173,969 offences of criminal damage.
ii. That figure was reduced by 50% to 586,985 to exclude the estimated number of offences committed against institutions and organisations. This was consistent with previous years and does not use data collected in the questionnaire to police forces as this was reckoned to underestimate the actual number of commercial offences against these targets.
iii. Under the counting rules in place before changes introduced in 1998, the number would have been reduced to 558,471.

Burglary (excluding attempts)

i. BTP numbers in this category are very small and are therefore not included in the unadjusted total of 307,122 offences of burglary in a dwelling.
ii. The total number of burglaries in a dwelling was reduced by 26.2% to 227,285 to account for 'nil value' burglaries (representing attempts). The proportion applied was from 2000 calculations as 'nil return' data is no longer collected centrally. No other adjustments were made.
iii. Under the counting rules in place before changes introduced in 1998, the number would have been increased to 227,319.

Attempted Burglary

i. The total number of attempted recorded crime burglaries in a dwelling was 79,837. This represents the 'nil value' offences within the burglary categories. No other adjustments were made.
ii. Under the counting rules in place before changes introduced in 1998, the number would have been increased to 79,861.

Theft From Motor Vehicle (Excluding Attempts)

i. Including BTP figures, the unadjusted total recorded crime figure was 491,134 offences of theft from a motor vehicle.
ii. This figure was reduced by 15.5% to 415,030 to account for 'nil value' thefts from motor vehicles (representing attempts).

iii. This total is then reduced by 12% to 366,377 to exclude thefts from commercial vehicles (proportion based on data from the 2005/06 questionnaire to police forces).
iv. Under the counting rules in place before changes introduced in 1998, the number would have been reduced to 363,722.

Theft of a Motor Vehicle

i. Including BTP figures, the unadjusted total recorded crime figure was 228,238 offences of theft of a motor vehicle.
ii. This figure was reduced by 25.8% to 169,429 to account for 'nil value' thefts from motor vehicles (representing attempts).
iii. This total is then reduced by 8% to 156,641 to exclude thefts of commercial vehicles (proportion based on data from the 2005/06 questionnaire to police forces).
iv. Under the counting rules in place before changes introduced in 1998, the number would have been reduced to 156,429.

Attempted Theft of and from a Motor Vehicle

i. 'Nil value' offences in the categories of theft of and theft from plus the number of vehicle tampering and interference offences brings the unadjusted total to 209,216 offences of attempted theft of and from a vehicle.
ii. This total is then reduced by 12% for attempted thefts from, 8% for attempted thefts of and 7% for vehicle tampering to 190,708 to exclude attempts on commercial vehicles (proportions based on data from the 2005/06 questionnaire to police forces).
iii. Vehicle tampering and interference was introduced in 1998 when recording rule changes were introduced, so no adjustments for that change are possible for this definition of attempted theft of and from a motor vehicle.

Bicycle Theft

i. Including BTP figures, the unadjusted total recorded crime figure was 108,845 offences of theft of a pedal cycle.
ii. This total is increased by 1.8% to 110,855 to take account of those thefts that are 'no crimes' by the police after a bicycle is recovered (these are still thefts of a bicycle on the BCS definition). It is not clear whether all police forces follow this procedure however.

iii. No adjustment has been made to allow for the very small proportion of thefts from bikes etc. recorded under the recorded crime classification 45.11 (theft from a vehicle other than a motor vehicle).
iv. Under the counting rules in place before changes introduced in 1998, the number would have been 107,941.

Wounding

i. Including BTP figures, the unadjusted total number of recorded crime offences for wounding was 539,023.
ii. This total was reduced by 11% to account for offences against those under 16 to stand at 477,157 offences (proportion based on data from the 2005/06 questionnaire to police forces).
iii. Under the counting rules in place before changes introduced in 1998, the number would have increased to 513,883.

Common Assault

i. Including BTP figures, the unadjusted total number of recorded crime offences for common assault was 220,655.
ii. This total was reduced by 20% to account for offences against those under 16 to stand at 175,487 offences (proportion based on data from the 2005/06 questionnaire to police forces).

Robbery

i. The unadjusted total number of recorded crime offences for robbery was 83,584.
ii. This total was reduced by 22% to account for offences against those under 16 to stand at 65, 572 offences (proportion based on data from 2005/06 questionnaire to police forces).
iii. Under the counting rules in place before changes introduced in 1998, the number would have decreased to 64,923.

Theft from the Person

i. Including BTP figures, the unadjusted total number of recorded crime offences for theft from the person was 122,396.
ii. This total was reduced by 7% to account for offences against those under 16 to stand at 114,245 offences (proportion based on data from 2005/06 questionnaire to police forces).
iii. Counting rules in place before changes introduced in 1998 would not have changed this figure.

Comparisons of crime data based on general population surveys with criminal statistics in Switzerland

Sandrine Haymoz, Marcelo F. Aebi, Martin Killias, Philippe Lamon

This contribution presents the available Swiss research on comparisons of criminal statistics and crime victim surveys. In the first part, we introduce the data that are going to be analysed. In the second part, we introduce the main studies that have performed this kind of comparisons. The third part includes a discussion on methodological issues. After that, we present the main results of these studies. Then, before the conclusions, we mentioned briefly how such comparisons have been used at the political and academic level.

I. Crime Data in Switzerland

1. Police statistics

In recent years, quite a few studies have analysed and criticised the current Swiss police statistics[1]. In this chapter, we follow the detailed description of them given by Eisner and Killias (2004).

Switzerland has 26 cantonal police forces and over 100 local police forces, many of which include less than 10 police officers. There is no national police force but a so-called Federal Police Office which coordinates local and cantonal activities and has limited competencies in areas such as state security, organised crime, drug trafficking and money laundering. National statistics on police-recorded crime were introduced in 1982. They are based on aggregated data supplied by the 26 cantonal police forces and the police forces of two major cities. They include data only on 21 selected Criminal Code offences with a clear majority of property offences, namely different kinds of theft. As these statistics are based on aggregated data, they are influenced by local specificities in the ways data are gathered and processed (Eisner, Killias, 2004).

1. See Fink (2005), Froidevaux (2005), and Killias (2005).

For example, some police forces count offences when they are reported or discovered by the police (*i.e. input* statistics), others count them when the police investigation is over (*i.e. output* statistics), and others count them at some point between these two moments (*i.e. intermediate* statistics). In that context, it has been shown empirically, at the international level, that the moment when data are registered for the statistics plays a major role in the total number of offences registered, with countries using input statistics presenting on average higher levels of police recorded crime than countries using output statistics (Aebi, 2008).
There are also differences in counting units and in the way multiple offences and continuous offences are recorded. For example, the 30 victims of a mass *suicide* of a sect in 1995 – many of whom were actually murdered – were counted as one *case* in the cantons of Valais and Fribourg, whereas the Zurich police probably would have recorded the total number of *victims*.
However, some cantons have developed more detailed statistics. Particularly important are the ones from the canton of Zurich, which registers approximately one-third of the offences that appear in the national statistics. Thus, in the following analyses, Zurich police statistics will be used to make reasonable estimates, whenever the federal statistics are insufficiently detailed.
Finally, it must be mentioned that, in 2010, a new set of police statistics will be introduced,.

2. National Crime Victim Survey Data

All the Swiss National Crime Victim Surveys were conducted by the School of Criminal Sciences of the University of Lausanne and directed by Martin Killias. The surveys took place in 1984/7, 1989, 1996, 1998, 2000, and 2005, and were all conducted through computer-assisted telephone interviews (CATI).
The first national crime survey of Switzerland was conducted in two phases in 1984 (French-speaking cantons) and in 1987 (German-speaking cantons and the Italian-speaking canton), with a sample of 6,505 respondents (Killias, 1989). The survey was one of the first major victim surveys conducted using CATI. The reference period was defined in a way that allowed victims to mention, in the first round, any victimisation that came to mind from the list mentioned by the interviewer. Then they were asked follow-up questions to determine more precisely the timing of the incident (*i.e.*, whether it took place during the current year, the previous year or earlier). These questions allowed telescoping to be reduced by

separating the definitional part of questions on offences from their temporal and spatial location. This structure was later included in the development of what became the International Crime Victim Survey or ICVS (van Dijk, Mayhew, Killias 1990). Since then, Swiss national victimisation surveys have followed the methodology of the ICVS – that combined several elements of former Dutch, British, Canadian and Swiss surveys – but have also benefited from innovative inputs. In particular, Switzerland participated in the ICVS of 1989, 1996, 2000 and 2005[2]. In 1989 and 1996, Switzerland opted for the standard sample of 1,000 randomly selected households. In 2000 and 2005, the samples were of 4,234 and 3,898 households respectively. Apart from that, in 1998, a national survey was conducted on a sample of 3,041 respondents following the methodology of the 1996 wave of the ICVS. In the surveys of 1998, 2000, and 2005, booster samples were taken from certain city areas in order to overrepresent the number of respondents from immigrant communities and allow a more detailed analysis of this group of the population.

The surveys of 1984, 1987, 1998 and 2005 were funded by the Swiss National Science Foundation. The surveys of 1989, 1996 were funded by the Justice Federal Office. Finally, the 2000 survey was funded by the Justice Federal Office, the Federal Police Office and the Federal Statistical Office.

II. Research on comparisons of Crime Statistics and Crime Surveys

Comparisons of crime statistics and crime victim surveys at the national level have been conducted by Killias, Lamon and Aebi (2004, 2005) and by Killias, Haymoz and Lamon (2007). Switzerland was also included in an international comparison of both sources (Aebi, Killias, Tavares, 2002). Comparisons of victim surveys, self reported-delinquency surveys, police records and court records at the individual level for a sample of approximately 500 hard-drug addicts following a heroin prescription program were conducted by Aebi (1999, 2006). Finally, comparisons of court statistics for juveniles and self-reported delinquency surveys were conducted by Killias, Lucia, Lamon and Simonin (2004).

2. See mainly van Dijk, Mayhew, Killias (1990), van Kesteren, Mayhew, Nieuwbeerta (2000), and van Dijk, van Kesteren, Smit (2007).

This report is based on the three first sources mentioned in the previous paragraph (Killias, Lamon, Aebi, 2004, 2005; Killias, Haymoz, Lamon, 2007) which include the most comprehensive comparisons conducted at the national level. They also correspond precisely to the goals of the CRIMPREV seminar on studies comparing crime data based on general population surveys with criminal statistics.

1. Methodology

In the following chapters, we compare victim surveys data and police data for a series of offences. Survey data were used to calculate two types of incidence rates: total number of victimisations and total number of victimisations reported to the police (*i.e.* number of offences and number of offences reported to the police). Depending on the type of offence, rates are expressed in offences per 1,000 respondents aged 16 or more, or per 1,000 households, or per 1,000 households owning a vehicle. Several adjustments were introduced to the data and they will be explained comprehensively in each chapter. Confidence intervals were calculated, but are not shown in the figures. Data are weighted and cover the period 1984-2005. In particular, data from the 1984 and the 1987 surveys were combined in order to produce national estimates, and they are presented under the heading 1985.

National police data were used to calculate police incidence rates. As mentioned before, whenever necessary, data were weighted according to Zurich police statistics – which provide a more detailed presentation of offences – in order to produce an adjusted police incidence rate. These adjustments are explained in the relevant chapters of this article.

Whenever possible, we tried to include only completed offences in our analyses. Rape is not included because the survey definition was enlarged in 1996 and, as a consequence, trend analyses are no longer possible.

Finally, in the following analyses, one must take into account that, according to the crime survey, from 1984 to 2005, reporting to the police diminished for property offences, including robbery, while reporting rates for assault and threats remained stable. This means that eventual increases in offences registered by police statistics do not reflect an increase in the victims' tendency to report such offences.

2. Results of the comparisons

Residential Burglary

Trends in residential burglary are presented in Figure 1. They include only completed burglaries (*i.e.* excluding attempts).

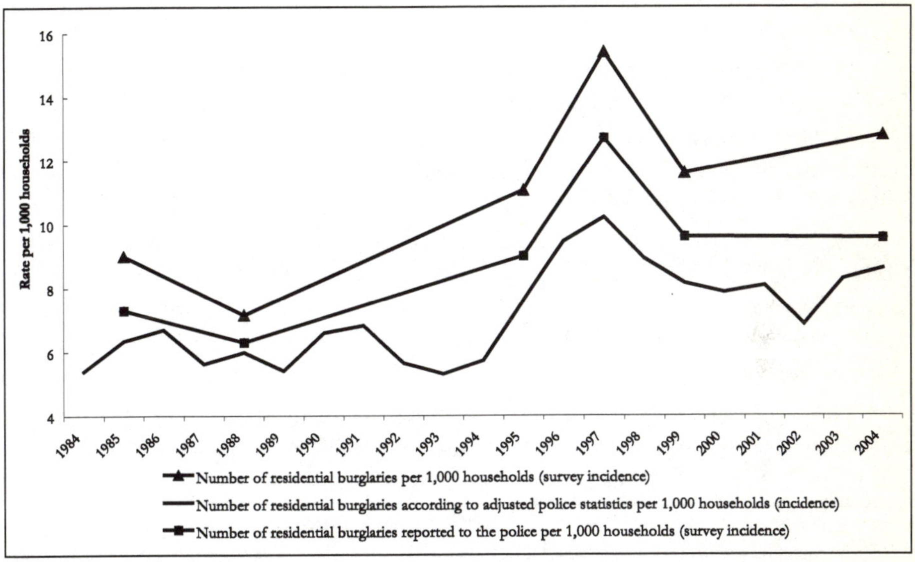

Figure 1: Trends in completed residential burglary rates per 1,000 households during one year according to the Swiss crime victim surveys and Swiss police statistics

In survey figures, burglaries from garages, sheds, cellars, lock-ups, and secondary residences were excluded. Prevalence and incidence rates per 1,000 households were calculated using demographic statistics and survey reporting rates were used to calculate rates of burglaries reported to the police per 1,000 households. The calculations implied replacing missing information through extrapolation. Thus, as in the 1989 and the 1996 surveys there were no questions on the frequency of cellar burglaries, the latter were estimated according to the 1984/7 survey – when they represented 35% of the total number of burglaries – and the 1998 and 2000 survey – when they represented 21% – respectively. Obviously, both surveys did not include questions on the number of cellar burglaries reported to the police neither. The problem comes from the fact that reporting rates are not the same for residential burglary and for cellar burglary. According to the 1984/7 survey, reporting rates were 92% for residential burglary and 74% for cellar burglaries. In that context, the 1989 figure for residential burglaries reported to the police was extrapolated using the reporting rates of the 1984/7 survey as a reference. The same was done for 1996 but using the average reporting rates of 1998 and 2000 as reference. Also, as the 1984/7 survey did not include the number of burglaries during the preceding year, their number was extrapolated according to the average of the other four surveys. However, the rate for the 1996 survey was extrapolated from the 1998 and 2000 surveys because there was an outlier among the respondents in 1996[3].

The federal police statistics give a higher burglary rate than the survey rate, because the federal police statistics category of burglary includes not only commercial burglaries, but also burglary from vending machines, telephone boxes, ticket machines, parking meters etc. For example, in 2004, there were 70,370 burglaries according to the federal statistics, which represents a rate of 21 burglaries per 1,000 households (in 2004, there were 3,232,191 households in Switzerland). That rate is largely higher than the ones of Swiss neighbouring countries[4]. Therefore, Zurich police statistics were used to weight the federal police data for the proportion of residential burglaries. In Zurich, 39.5% of the burglaries registered by the police were residential burglaries (in houses or apartments). Applying this percentage to the federal police statistics, the adjusted figure is 27,828 residential burglaries which correspond to a rate of 8.6 residential burglaries per 1'000 households.

Survey data and adjusted police data followed the same pattern during the period studied. However, the adjusted police rate is lower than what victims declared having reported to the police. The reason for this difference could be that the police probably do not record all offences reported to them and also, as suggested by Birrer and Ribaux (2008), that some offences recorded at the cantonal level are not included in the federal statistics. Apart from that, the comparison of prevalence rates (not shown here) and incidence rates according to the crime victim survey shows that from 2000 to 2005 the first one remained stable while the second one has increased. This means that there are more cases of repeated victimisation.

3. Thirteen out of 1,000 respondents mentioned that they had been victims of a burglary and one of these persons mentioned that her household had been victimised four times.
4. See Aebi *et al.* 2006, 48, Table 1.2.1.12.

Theft of motorcycles/mopeds/scooters and bicycles

Trends in theft of motorcycles and mopeds are presented in Figure 2, while trends in thefts of bicycles are presented in Figure 3.

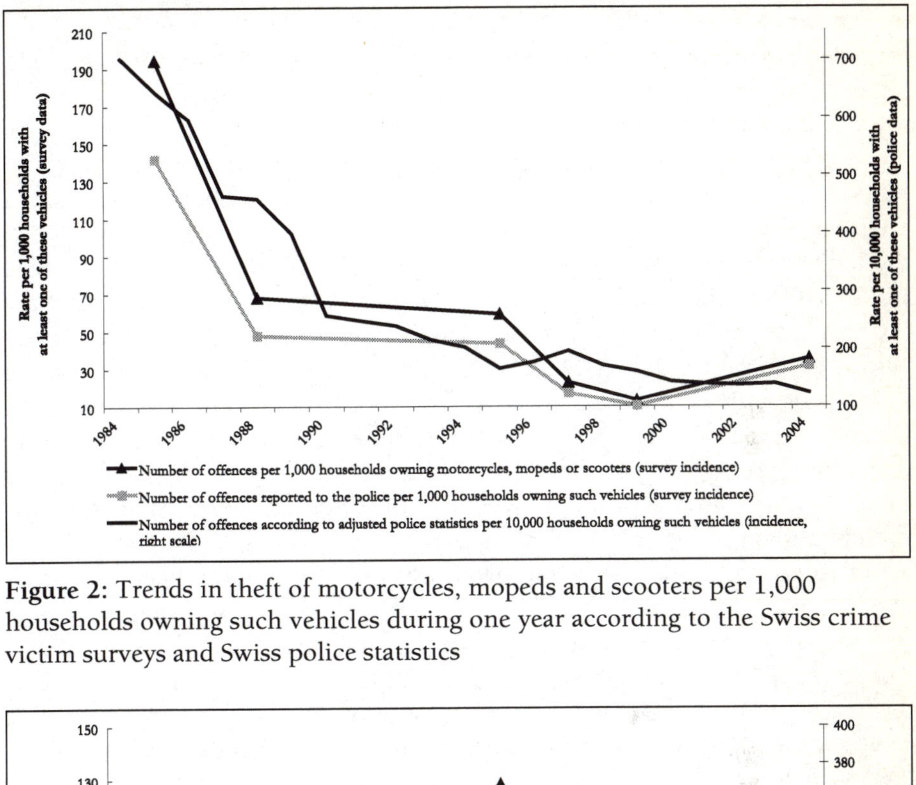

Figure 2: Trends in theft of motorcycles, mopeds and scooters per 1,000 households owning such vehicles during one year according to the Swiss crime victim surveys and Swiss police statistics

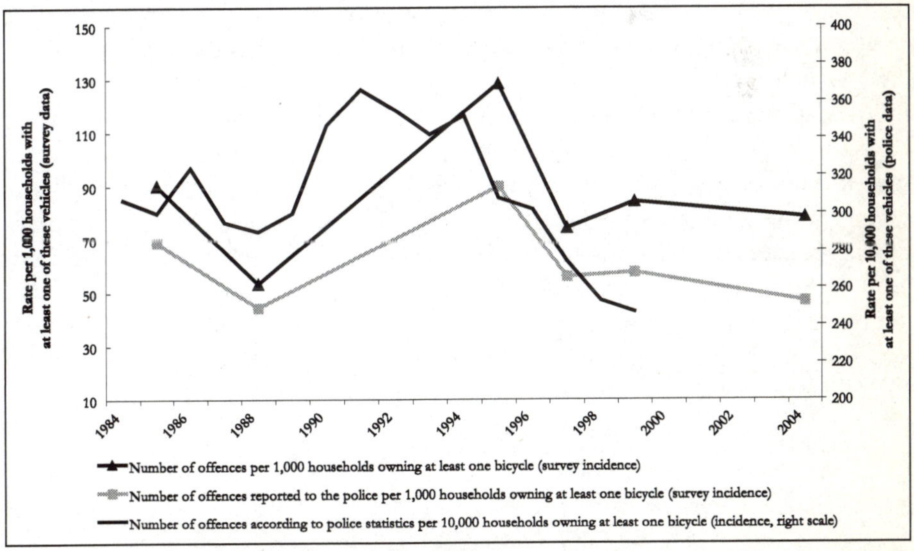

Figure 3: Trends in theft of bicycles per 1,000 households owning a bicycle during one year according to the Swiss crime victim surveys and Swiss police statistics

The survey questionnaire included screening questions on the possession of motorcycles, mopeds and scooters as well as bicycles. These screening questions were used to estimate the number of households owning such vehicles and therefore incidence rates were calculated taking that number of households as a reference. All surveys except the one from 2000 included questions on the frequency of such thefts, which allow measuring repeated victimisation. As a consequence, the average of all other surveys was used to weight the figures for 2000. As an example, in the case of motorcycles, mopeds and scooters, a weight of 1.33 was applied to the 10 households that admitted such a crime in 2000, producing an adjusted incidence rate of 13 thefts for 1,000 households owning a motorcycle, moped or bicycle. Police figures come from an unpublished police database called RIPOL. The screening questions of the survey were used to estimate the number of households owning such vehicles. Thus, incidence rates were calculated taking that number of households as a reference. As the number of thefts registered by the police was considerably lower than the number of thefts reported by the victims, the first number –thefts registered by the police– is presented as a rate per 10,000 instead of 1,000 inhabitants (right scale) in order to produce a figure that remains understandable.

The striking difference between the absolute number of offences according to police and survey data may be explained by the fact that cheap vehicles and vehicles recovered quickly are not included in the RIPOL database. Apart from that, the *trends* for both indicators are comparable. The dramatic drop in the survey rate of theft of motorcycles, mopeds and scooters during the late 1980s, was probably influenced by a change in the law, which made compulsory the wearing of helmets[5] and limited the modifications that the owner could introduced to his/her vehicle. Police data show a similar trend, though it is less pronounced, possibly because minor incidents often went unrecorded, particularly during the 1980s, when many vehicles were located rapidly. The reduction in the popularity of mopeds among juveniles is likely to have affected joy-riding more than actual theft. That factor could explain why police data shows a slight decrease in recent years. Indeed, cases when the vehicle is recovered quickly, as in the case of joy-riding, are not necessarily included in the RIPOL database.

5. A similar effect was found by Mayhew, Clarke and Elliott (1989) in the United Kingdom.

Robbery

Trends in robbery are presented in Figure 4.

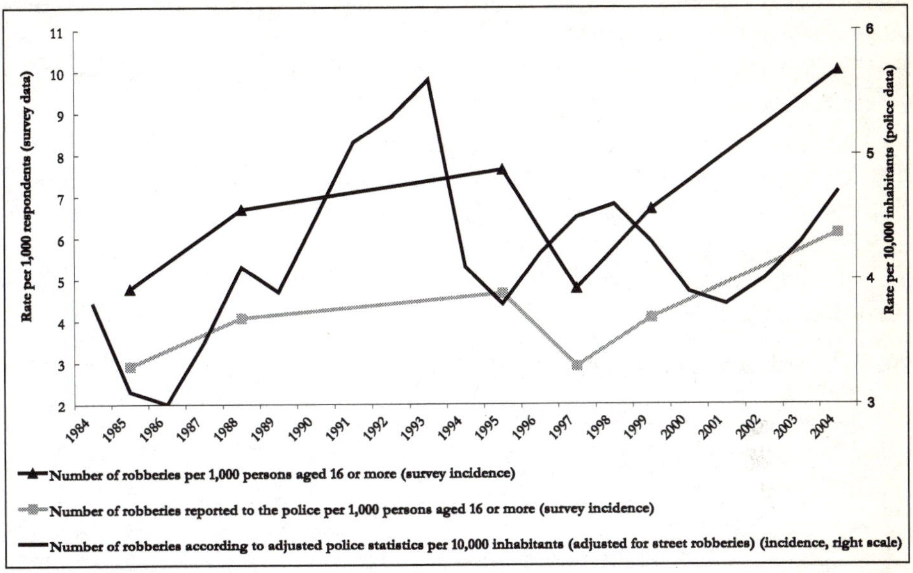

Figure 4: Trends in robberies per 1,000 persons during one year according to the Swiss crime victim surveys and Swiss police statistics

Survey data include attempts and refer to street robberies as well as bag-snatching and other forms of *mugging*. However, even with relatively large samples, the number of robberies experienced in Switzerland is not large enough to provide reliable annual rates, especially as far as robberies reported to the police are concerned. In order to reduce this problem, the annual rates were combined with the last five years rates. In that context, for the six surveys, there were on average 32 persons per 1,000 that suffered a robbery during the last year, and 85 during the last five years. This produces an average rapport of 2.66 (85/32). Thus, 5 years prevalence rates were divided by 2.66 in order to produce an annual rate that would be less dependent on the size of the samples.

As it has been said, survey definitions of robbery include bag-snatching and other forms of mugging. In Switzerland, such offences are legally considered as forms of theft. However, in order to adjust police measures to survey indicators, they were also included in the total number of robberies. On the other hand, commercial robberies were excluded, using detailed information from Zurich police statistics – indeed, only robberies committed in public places (streets) were included– and weighting the federal data accordingly. Whereas survey measures include only incidents experienced by persons aged 16 or over, the police data (and related population figures) refer to the total population because is not possible to exclude from the police figures the incidents experienced by victims of less than 16 years. Finally, as the number of robberies registered by the police was considerably lower than the number of thefts reported by the victims, the first number – thefts registered by the police – is presented as a rate per 10,000 instead of 1,000 inhabitants.

Survey and police data show similar trends, however the trends are displaced in time due to the use of the five year weighing procedure. Moreover the number of cases registered by the police is extremely low compared to survey figures.

Assault and threats

Assault and threats are presented in Figure 5.

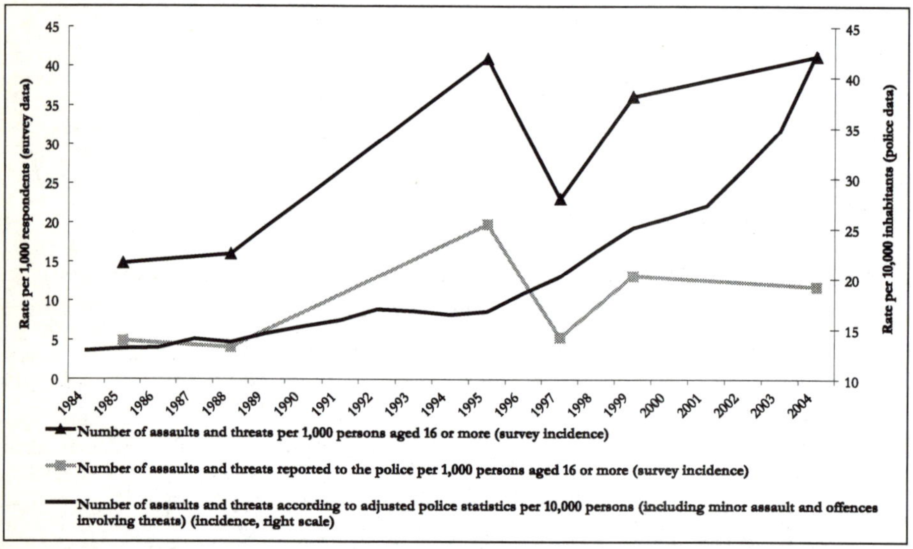

Figure 5: Trends in assaults and threats per 1,000 persons during one year according to the Swiss crime victim surveys and Swiss police statistics

Survey measures are annual rates of assault and threats. As the 1989 did not include the number of cases suffered abroad, the figure for that year was increased by 2% (*i.e.* the percentage of offences suffered abroad according to the rest of the surveys).

Police data include first, second, and third-degree cases of bodily-injury, but also threats, extortions and deprivation of liberty, in order to reach a maximum of consistency with survey measures of assault (which could include experiences legally qualifying for any of these criminal code sections). Since police measures are by far lower than survey estimates for assault and threats, it was decided to include robberies in police data, assuming that some victims might have indicated attempted robberies or muggings under the heading of assaults and threats. Finally, as the number of robberies registered by the police was considerably lower than the number of thefts reported by the victims, the first number – thefts registered by the police – is presented as a rate per 10,000 instead of 1,000 inhabitants.

Despite the inclusion of a number of related offences which might be listed under the survey measure of assault, the gap between police data and survey measures seems dramatic. This is due undoubtedly to the fact that second and third-degree bodily injuries are prosecuted on the formal request of the victim only. In practice, this probably leads the police to record offences only when the suspect is known and when the victim really insists on his or her prosecution[6]. Switzerland is indeed one of the countries where, in the case of assault, the number of suspects matches by and large the number of recorded offences, whereas in countries where recording occurs at an earlier stage, the number of offences typically exceeds by far the number of suspects[7]. Moreover, during the first half of the 1990s, there were many open drug scenes in Switzerland and, according to different police sources, a conservative policy of recording personal offences was applied in that context. Thus, for that period, police recorded offences are probably artificially low. As a consequence, it is not surprising that the massive trend changes indicated by survey measures between 1995 and 1999 are not reflected in police statistics. Nevertheless, globally, survey and police data show an overall increase in assault and threats between 1984 and 2005. Yet, there are great variations when shorter periods are studied. As it has been explained before, these results suggest that police record only a small part of the robberies reported.

6. An observational study conducted in Southern Germany thirty years ago (Kürzinger, 1978) has shown that theft is recorded in over 90 % of cases, while that rate drops to 30 % for cases of assault. In the same perspective, recent research in England and Wales has shown that the police record less than 40 % of the reported offences against the person (Burrows, Tarling, Mackie, Lewis, Taylor, 2000). Switzerland is surely not an exception to this rule.
7. See, Aebi *et al.* 2006, 42, 57, Tables 1.2.1.6 and 1.2.2.5.

III. Use of the comparisons

At the international level, two of the articles presented here (Killias, Lamon, Aebi, 2004, 2005), were part of a joint research organised by the Institute of Criminology of Cambridge of the University of Cambridge and the US Department of Justice. That research lasted a few years and showed that, in continental Europe, only the Netherlands, Switzerland and Sweden were able to provide longitudinal reliable data for comparisons between survey and police data with the level of detail required by a severe protocol of the research[8].

In Switzerland, the methodology used for these three articles did not create any political or academic debate. On the contrary, the *trends* showed in all these articles led to a controversy with researchers that considered that delinquency had not changed during all these years.

*

The fact that Switzerland has national police statistics based on aggregated data and covering only a few offences makes comparisons with crime victim surveys extremely difficult. Only three studies conducted by the academics that were involved in the organization of the Swiss national crime victim surveys have tried to make such comparisons. In that context, national police statistics were weighted according to the Zurich police statistics, which represent one third of the offences included in the national statistics, in order to obtain detailed national figures for some offences.

The comparison shows that the absolute number of offences varies widely from survey to police data. As expected, survey figures are always higher than police figures, and that is the case even when only reported offences to the police (according to victims statements) are compared. However, as both sources are not strictly comparable, it is not possible to conclude that victim surveys provide a real estimate of the dark figure. Indeed, it is more interesting to compare crime trends according to police and survey data. When such comparisons are performed, one can see that in the long run (1984 to 2005, *i.e.* 21 years) the trends are more or less similar. However, large variations can be observed.

In sum, given the particularities of the Swiss crime data, comparisons of police statistics and victim surveys seem useful for estimating crime trends for long periods of time, but they are not useful for establishing actual levels of crime or for analyzing crime trends for short periods of time.

8. Farrington, Langan, Tonry (2004); Tonry, Farrington (2005).

References

AEBI M. F., 1999, *La validité des indicateurs de la criminalité*. Lausanne, University of Lausanne, Ph.d. Dissertation.

AEBI M. F., 2006, *Comment mesurer la délinquance ?* Paris, Armand Colin.

AEBI M.F., 2008, Measuring the Influence of Statistical Counting Rules on Cross-National Differences in Recorded Crime, *in* AROMAA K., HEISKANEN M., (Eds.). *Crime and Criminal Justice Systems in Europe and North America 1995-2004*, HEUNI Publication Series No. 55. Helsinki, HEUNI, 196-214, Also available online at: [http://www.heuni.fi/43087.htm].

AEBI M. F., AROMAA K., AUBUSSON DE CAVARLAY B., BARCLAY G., GRUSZCZYNSKA B., VON HOFER H., HYSI V., JEHLE J.-M., KILLIAS M., SMIT P., TAVARES C., 2006, *European Sourcebook of Crime and Criminal Justice Statistics 2006*, Den Haag, Home Office, Swiss Federal Statistical Office, Cesdip, Boom Juridische uitgevers, Wetenschappelijk Onderzoek- en Documentatiecentrum. Also available online at: [http://www.europeansourcebook.org].

AEBI M. F., KILLIAS M., TAVARES C., 2002, Comparing Crime Rates: The International Crime (Victim) Survey, the European Sourcebook of Crime and Criminal Justice Statistics, and Interpol Statistics, *International Journal of Comparative Criminology*, 2, 1, 22–37.

BIRRER S., RIBAUX O., 2008, La statistique policière de la criminalité en Suisse peut-elle s'envisager dans le cadre du renseignement criminel ? *Revue Suisse de Criminologie*, 7, 2, 13-20.

BURROWS J., TARLING R., MACKIE A., LEWIS R., TAYLOR G., 2000, *Review of police forces crime recording practices*, Londres, Home Office.

EISNER M., KILLIAS M., 2004, Switzerland. *European Journal of Criminology*, 1, 2, 257-293.

FARRINGTON D. P., LANGAN P. A., TONRY M. (Eds.), 2004, *Cross-National Studies in Crime and Justice*, Washington, Bureau of Justice Statistics.

FINK D., 2005, Stand und Perspektiven der Kriminalstatistik, *Revue Suisse de Criminologie*, 2, 34–40.

FROIDEVAUX D., 2005, L'impossible statistique policière de la criminalité ?, *Revue Suisse de Criminologie*, 2, 53–57.

KILLIAS M., 1989, *Les Suisses face au crime: Leurs expériences et attitudes à la lumière des sondages suisses de victimisation*. Grüsch (Grisons), Rüegger.

KILLIAS M., 2005, Une collecte véritablement professionnelle des données, *Revue Suisse de Criminologie*, 2, 41–43.

KILLIAS M., LAMON P., AEBI M.F., 2004, Crime and Punishment in Switzerland *in* Farrington D.P, LANGAN P.A., TONRY M. (Eds.), *Cross-*

National Studies in Crime and Justice, Washington DC, Bureau of Justice Statistics, 239–278.

KILLIAS M., LAMON P., AEBI M.F., 2005, Crime and Punishment in Switzerland, 1985–1999 *in* TONRY M., FARRINGTON D. P. (Ed.), *Crime and Punishment in Western Countries, 1980–1999. Crime and Justice: A Review of Research,* Chicago/London, University of Chicago Press, 213-245.

KILLIAS M., HAYMOZ S., LAMON PH., 2007, *Swiss Crime Survey*, Berne, Stämpfli.

KILLIAS M., LUCIA S., LAMON PH., SIMONIN M., 2004, Juvenile delinquency in Switzerland over 50 years: Assessing trends beyond statistics, *European Journal on Criminal Policy and Research*, 10, 2, 111–122.

KÜRZINGER J., 1978, *Private Strafanzeige und polizeiliche Reaktion*, Berlin, Duncker & Humblot.

MAYHEW P., CLARKE R.V., ELLIOTT D., 1989, Motorcycle Theft, Helmet Legislation and Displacement, *The Howard Journal*, 28, 1, 1–8.

TONRY M., FARRINGTON D. P. (Ed.), 2005, *Crime and Punishment in Western Countries, 1980–1999.* Chicago/London, University of Chicago Press.

VAN DIJK J. J. M., MAYHEW P., KILLIAS M., 1990, *Experiences of crime across the world*, Deventer NL/Boston, Kluwer.

VAN DIJK J., VAN KESTEREN J., SMIT P., 2007, *Criminal Victimisation in International Perspective*, Universiteit Tilburg.

VAN KESTEREN J., MAYHEW P., NIEUWBEERTA P., 2000, *Criminal Victimisation in Seventeen Industrialised Countries. Key finding from the 2000 International Crime Victims Survey*, The Hague, WODC, Ministry of Justice.

On the authors

Marcelo F. Aebi is Professor of Criminology and Vice-director of the School of Criminal Sciences at the University of Lausanne, Switzerland. He is also Associate Professor at the Autonomous University of Barcelona, Spain. He has been a visiting fellow at the Rutgers School of Criminal Justice (New Jersey, United States of America) and at the Max Planck Institute for Foreign and International Criminal Law (Freiburg, Germany) as well as Vice-director and Professor of Criminology at the Andalusian Institute of Criminology of the University of Seville (Spain). Currently, he is also a consultant expert of the Council of Europe and the European Commission, as well as the Executive Secretary of the European Society of Criminology.

His main research topics include juvenile delinquency, comparative criminology, corrections, methodology, drugs and crime, and victimisation and self-reported delinquency studies.

His most recent books are

- *Temas de criminología*, Madrid, Dykinson, 2008.
- *Comment mesurer la délinquance*, Paris, Armand Colin, 2006.

He is also one of the co-authors of the

- *European Sourcebook of Crime and Criminal Justice Statistics,* 3rd edition, The Hague, Boom Juridische Uitgevers, 2006.

Bruno Aubusson de Cavarlay, *directeur de recherches* at the *Centre national de la recherche scientifique* (CNRS), is a member of *Centre de recherche sur le droit et les institutions pénales* (CESDIP).

His main research topics include criminal statistics and the functioning of the criminal justice system. He conducted quantitative surveys describing the penal tracks along this system and long term analysis based on the French *Compte général de la Justice Criminelle* (1831-1978). He is a member of the experts group European Sourcebook of Crime and Criminal Statistics.

Among his recent publications:

- Affaires traitées par la justice pénale : les cas de violence selon les catégories de la statistique criminelle (France, 1831-1932), *in* Follain A., Lemesle B., Nassiet M., Pierre E., Quincy-Lefebre P., (Dir.), *La violence et le judiciaire. Discours, perceptions, pratiques*, Rennes, Presses universitaires de Rennes, 223-240.
- Des comptes rendus à la statistique criminelle : c'est l'unité qui compte (France, XIXe-XXe siècles), *Histoire & Mesure*, 2007, XXII, 2, 39-73.

- The Prosecution Service Function within the French Criminal Justice System, *in* Jehle J.M., Wade M., (Eds.), *Coping with Overloaded Criminal Justice Systems, The Rise of Prosecutorial Power across Europe*, Berlin/ Heidelberg, Springer, 2006, 185-206.
- *European Sourcebook of Crime and Criminal Justice Statistics*, 3rd edition, WODC, Den Haag, Boom Juridische Uitgevers, 2006, (with M.F. Aebi, K. Aromaa, G. Barclay, B. Gruszczyñska, H. von Hofer, V. Hysi, J.M. Jehle, M. Killias, P. Smit and C. Tavarès).
- Crime trends in the EU, *European Journal on Criminal Policy and Research*, 2004, 10, 187•223 (with Chris Lewis, Gordon Barclay, Maria Joáo Morgado Costa and Paul Smit).

Sandrine Haymoz is a psychologist-criminologist and a PhD Student of Criminology at the School of Criminal Sciences at the University of Lausanne. She also teaches at the University of Applied Sciences in Social Work in Fribourg.
Her main research topics include juvenile delinquency, especially juvenile gangs, self-reported victimisation and delinquency studies.
She is co-author, with Martin Killias and Philippe Lamon, of the book
La criminalité en Suisse et son évolution à la lumière des sondages de victimisation de 1984 à 2005, Berne, Stämpfli, 2007
and has published several articles on juvenile delinquency.

Mike Hough is Director of the Institute for Criminal Policy Research in the School of Law at King's College London. ICPR has a staff of 12, carrying out policy research for government, criminal justice agencies and for independent funders.
He has published extensively on a range of criminological topics including policing, crime prevention and community safety, anti-social behaviour, probation and drugs. Current work includes research on sentencing, on drugs, on youth justice and on public trust in justice. He is the President of the British Society of Criminology.
Recent publications include:

- Hough M., Hunter G., Jacobson J., Cossalter S., 2008, *The impact of the Licensing Act 2003 on levels of crime and disorder: an evaluation.* Home Office Research Report 04, London, Home Office.
- Hough M., Jacobson, J., 2008, *Creating a Sentencing Commission for England and Wales: an opportunity to address the prisons crisis,* London, Prison Reform Trust.
- Hough M., Roberts J.V., Jacobson, J., Bredee A., Moon, N., 2008, *Attitudes to the sentencing of offences involving death by driving,* Sentencing Advisory Panel Report No. 5, London, Sentencing Advisory Panel.

- Hough M, Allen R., Solomon E., (Eds), 2008, *Tackling Prison Overcrowding*, Bristol, Policy Press.
- Hough M., Maxfield M., (Eds.), 2007, *Surveying Crime in the 21st Century,* Cullompton, Willan Publishing.

Martin Killias is Professor of Criminology and Criminal Law at the Law Faculty of the University of Zurich. He used to be Professor at the School of Criminal Sciences at the University of Lausanne from 1982 to 2006. Trained in Sociology and Law, he received his PhD from the University of Zurich in 1979. He served as a post-doctoral fellow at the School of Criminal Justice of the State University of New York at Albany, and as a visiting professor in several universities in the United States, in Canada, the Netherlands, and Italy.
He initiated the Swiss Crime Surveys in 1984 and remained responsible for all subsequent crime surveys since then. Martin Killias was also among the authors of the first international crime victimisation survey conducted in 1989. Later initiatives include the European Sourcebook of Crime and Criminal Justice Statistics (chair since 1993) and the foundation of the European Society of Criminology (first president, 2000-2001). He was also associated with the first and second international surveys on self-reported juvenile delinquency (conducted in 1992 and 2006).

Philippe Lamon is Child Protection Agent in the Swiss canton of Valais. He has been consultant at the United Nations Office on Drugs and Crime and research assistant at the University of Lausanne.
His main research topics include feelings of insecurity, crime trends, victimisation and self-reported delinquency studies.
He is co-author, with Martin Killias and Sandrine Haymoz, of the book *La criminalité en Suisse et son évolution à la lumière des sondages de victimisation de 1984 à 2005*, Berne, Stämpfli, 2007.

Paul Norris. Having recently completed his doctoral studies in Social Policy (University of Edinburgh), he is a Research Fellow in the Scottish Centre for Crime and Justice Research.
His primary interest is the use of quantitative methods in criminology, and in particular the use of comparative approaches to research. He works extensively on the relationship between and individual's social context and their experience of crime and justice. This research regularly involves the use of crime survey data from within Scotland, across the UK more generally and from the International Crime Victim Survey.
His recent publications include
Public Order Expenditure Across Industrialised Countries, *in* Castles F., (Ed.), *The Disappearing State?*, Cheltenham, Edward Elgar, 2007.

Joachim Obergfell-Fuchs is a psychologist, Head of the Criminological Service in the Baden-Wuerttemberg Department of Corrections.
His main research topics are evaluation within the correctional system, sex offenders, sanctioning, crime prevention, forensics.
Among his recent publications:

- Evaluation des Strafvollzugs, *Forum Strafvollzug*, 2008, 57, 5, 231-236 (with R. Wulf).
- 'Punitivity' within the criminal justice system in Germany *in* Kury H., (Ed.), *Fear of crime – punitivity. New developments in theory and research*, Bochum, Universitätsverlag Dr. N. Brockmeyer, 2008, 303-320.
- Crime victims and insecurity surveys in Germany *in* Zauberman R., (Ed.), *Victimisation and insecurity in Europe. A review of surveys and their use*, Brussels, VUBPress, 2008, 105-125.

Philippe Robert is a sociologist, *Dr h.c. mult.*, *Directeur de recherches émérite* at the *Centre national de la recherche scientifique* (CNRS). He is the founder and former head of the *Centre de recherches sociologiques sur le droit et les institutions pénales* (CESDIP), the main French research centre on crime. He has also founded the *Groupe européen de recherches sur les normativités* (GERN), an European scientific network. Within the Coordination Action CRIMPREV, he coordinated the workshop of which this volume is one of the outcomes.
His current fields of research are the sociological theory of crime, measuring crime, victimisation and insecurity surveys.
Among his recent publications:

- *Sociologia do crime,* Petropolis, Vozes (www.editoravozes.com.br), 2007.
- *Sociologie du crime*, Paris, La Découverte (www.editionsladecouverte.fr), Coll. Repères, 2005.
- *Bürger, Kriminalität und Staat*, Wiesbaden, VS Verlag für Sozialwissenschaften/GmbH (www.vs-verlag.de), 2005.

Giovanni Sacchini, sociologist, works for the local government of the Regione Emilia-Romagna, where is in charge of the statistical activities in the office for the Policies of Urban safety (*Città sicure*). He also collaborate with the University of Ferrara teaching *Elementi di Criminologia.*
As a researcher, he has conducted research in the field of the diffusion of crime (working with administrative data) and in the field of victimisation and perception of insecurity, using in this case data from surveys.
Recently he has been editor of
Quindici anni di delittuosità e percezione della sicurezza nelle regioni italiane: 1991- 2006, FISU 2008)
and has published the article

Motivi che aiutano a violare le norme. Alcuni suggerimenti ricavati da un'indagine tra gli studenti bolognesi, *Metronomie*, 2007, XIV, 34-35.

Jan Van Dijk holds the Pieter van Vollenhoven Chair in Victimology, Human Security and Safety at the University of Tilburg, The Netherlands. His former posts include director of crime prevention at the Dutch Ministry of Justice and officer in charge of the United Nations crime prevention programme in Vienna. In 2003 he received the Hans von Hentig Award from the World Society of Victimology and in 2008 the Sellin-Glueck Award from the American Society of Criminology. He is an Officer in the Order of Oranje-Nassau.
His latest book is *The World of Crime; breaking the silence on issues of security, justice and development*, Sage Publications, CA, 2008.

Karin Wittebrood is a senior researcher at the Netherlands Institute of Social Research (*Sociaal en Cultureel Planbureau,* SCP).
Her interests are on criminal victimisation and fear of crime, the impact of social context on these issues and the effectiveness of policy measures to reduce (fear of) crime.
Recent publications have appeared in *The British Journal of Criminology, European Sociological Review, Homicide Studies* and *Social Problems.*

Renée Zauberman is a senior researcher at the *Centre de recherches sociologiques sur le droit et les institutions pénales*, a research centre affiliated to the French *Centre National de la Recherche scientifique,* the *Université de Versailles Saint Quentin* (UVSQ) and the French Department of Justice.
Her interest lies is norms and deviance, especially criminal justice and crime. While she has worked on the French Gendarmerie, her current focus is on victimisation surveys.
She has recently published:

- L'acteur et la mesure. Le comptage de la délinquance entre données administratives et enquêtes *Revue Française de sociologie*, 2009, 50, 1, 31-62 (with Philippe Robert, Sophie Névanen and Emmanuel Didier).
- L'évolution de la délinquance d'après les enquêtes de victimation. France, 1984-2005, *Déviance & Société,* 2008, 32, 4, 435-472 (with Ph. Robert, S. Névanen, E. Didier)
- Police, Minorities and the French Republican Ideal, *Criminology*, 2003, 41, 4, 1065-1100 (with R. Lévy).

And edited
Victimisation and Insecurity in Europe. A review of Surveys and their Use, Brussels, VUBPress, 2008.